SHOPPING GUIDE FOR CARING CONSUMERS

SHOPPING GUIDE FOR

CARING
CONSUMERS

A GUIDE TO PRODUCTS THAT ARE NOT TESTED ON ANIMALS

PEOPLE FOR THE ETHICAL TREATMENT OF ANIMALS

BOOK PUBLISHING COMPANY
SUMMERTOWN, TENNESSEE

PETA attempts to update this guide annually. However, we may not receive necessary information before going to print. Therefore, this guide is based on the most current information available at the time of printing. Companies not listed as cruelty-free may be cruelty-free but are not included because they have not sent PETA a letter stating their complete rejection of animal testing, nor signed PETA's statement of assurance. Companies identified as conducting animal tests may have changed their animal-testing policies after this edition was printed. Inclusion on any list is not an endorsement of a company and/or any of its products by PETA. For periodically updated company information, please contact PETA.

PETA's updated 2000 *Shopping Guide for Caring Consumers* lists more than 550 cruelty-free cosmetics, household, and personal-care product companies, making it easy to find everything from hair color and furniture polish to correction fluid and more.

© 1999 PETA   ISBN 1-57067-089-7

The Book Publishing Company
P.O. Box 99
Summertown, TN 38483

Edited by Susan Rayfield
Proofread by Karen Porreca
and Julia Craig Mundy

PETA
People for the Ethical Treatment of Animals
501 Front St.
Norfolk, VA 23510
757-622-PETA
www.peta-online.org

TABLE OF CONTENTS

Foreword 6
A Special Message from Alicia Silverstone 7
Corporate Standard of Compassion for Animals 9
Blinding Bunnies and Poisoning Dogs 9
V is for Vegan 10
Look For the New Logo 10
Companies That Don't Test On Animals 11
Catalogs/Stores Offering Cruelty-Free Products 77
Quick Reference Guide.. 78
    Air Freshener 78
    Aromatherapy 78
    Baby Care 79
    Baking Soda 79
    Bleach.. 79
    Car Care 79
    Carpet Cleaning 79
    Companion Animal Care 79
    Condoms/Lubricants 80
    Contact Lens Solution 80
    Cosmetics... 80
    Dandruff Shampoo 81
    Dental Hygiene 81
    Deodorant.. 81
    Ethnic Products 82
    Feminine Hygiene 82
    Fragrances for Men 82
    Fragrances for Women 82
    Furniture Polish 83
    Hair Care 83
    Hair Color 84
    Household Products 85
    Hypo-Allergenic Skin Care 85
    Insect Repellant/Treatment 86
    Laundry Detergent.. 86
    Laundry Detergent for Fine Washables.............. 86
    Makeup Brush (Vegan).................................. 86
    Nail Care 86
    Office Supplies 86
    Paint 87
    Permanents 87
    Razors 87
    Shaving Supply 87
    Skin Care.. 87
    Sun Care/Tanning 89
    Theatrical Makeup 90
    Toiletries/Personal Care 90
    Toothbrushes 91
    Vitamins/Herbs 91
Companies That Test on Animals............................ 94
Alternatives to Leather and Other Animal Products .. 99
Health Charities: Helping or Hurting? 101
Health Charities That Don't Test on Animals 102
Health Charities That Test on Animals.................... 112
Company Coupons 117
What Is PETA?.. 127

FOREWORD

This tenth edition of the *Shopping Guide for Caring Consumers* is a special one. As we celebrate the new millennium, we also reflect upon the past decade—we've made enormous strides toward ending product testing on animals. Only a wink in time ago, it seemed the only place to find non-animal-tested products was in health food stores. Now, thanks to caring consumers like you, cruelty-free personal care and household products line the shelves at supermarkets, department stores, and drugstores everywhere.

Our list of cruelty-free companies has grown to include more than 550 companies, including The Body Shop, Mary Kay, Estée Lauder, and Revlon. These companies have signed PETA's statement of assurance or the Corporate Standard of Compassion for Animals. They've put their commitment in writing, guaranteeing that they do not (and never will) test ingredients or finished products on animals.

The list of vegan companies (those that use alternatives to animal testing *and* animal ingredients) has grown, too. Many of these companies proudly advertise on their labels that they use no lanolin, beeswax, or other animal ingredients—and with our list, it's easier than ever for you to buy only vegan cosmetics and household products. Also, to help you find stylish, comfortable alternatives to leather shoes, belts, handbags, and other accessories, this guide includes "Alternatives to Leather and Other Animal Products." It's a cinch to take the "moo" out of your shoes!

Our "Health Charities" section is included to help you decide which charities deserve your support. Many compassionate people refuse to support charities that blind, burn, mutilate, or otherwise use and kill animals in cruel animal experiments. On this list, you'll find many caring charities that help people without hurting animals.

We admire and appreciate your efforts to make this a kinder world for animals. The extra cents you may spend for a cruelty-free lipstick make a strong statement—that you refuse to participate in the killing of animals in Draize eye, skin irritancy, and lethal dose tests. Caring consumers like you are helping to ensure that more companies will abandon animal tests, choosing instead to use effective, humane alternatives such as tissue and cell cultures and computer models. As the demand for cruelty-free products grows, so will their availability.

Again, thanks for your concern and respect for animals and your commitment to cruelty-free living.

I cannot begin to tell you how excited I am that this book has found its way into your hands. As soon as I started using it, I felt an enormous weight lifted from me, and with that came the pride and satisfaction of knowing that I could make a difference. Once you see the difference that this book can make in your life and the lives of thousands of animals, I'm sure you will feel the same way.

With every purchase that we make, we are making a choice. We can either sponsor cruel, torturous, needless animal testing that destroys countless lives each year or use our dollars to support companies that have proved that it's possible to make superior products without resorting to barbaric methods and putting their financial bottom line before the most basic rights of all creatures. I choose the latter.

Everything you need to know is right here, conveniently categorized for easy reference, which is just one of the reasons why this book is so great.

Although in the beginning it may seem a bit daunting to consult this guide every time you want to buy a household or personal care product, once you make the transition to a cruelty-free lifestyle you'll be surprised at how quickly you get the hang of it. You will probably find that some of the products you are already using are cruelty-free, whereas some other great less-well-known products will be new to you. It won't be long before you find a few that you love and then this guide will serve as more of a reference list.

In the meantime, if you need a few recommendations to get you started, I am particularly fond of Kiehl's, The Body Shop, Jurlique, and Dermalogica for facial and skin-care products such as scrubs, masks, moisturizer, and body lotions. I also like Kiehl's for shampoo and conditioner, as well as Paul Mitchell, Aveda, and Sebastian. For household products, the *Shopping Guide for Caring Consumers* introduced me to a terrific company called Seventh Generation that makes everything from feminine hygiene products to dishwashing liquid and from laundry detergent to baby-wipes. I also use Bon Ami products for a variety of purposes around the house.

These are just a few of the products that I have found work well for me. However, I invite you to find your own favorites. As you'll discover, it's a great feeling to enjoy affordable high-quality products, knowing that a fellow living creature did not suffer horrific atrocities in order to make them. You can make a difference.

Thanks for caring!

Alicia Silverstone

THE SHOPPING GUIDE FOR CARING CONSUMERS

People for the Ethical Treatment of Animals (PETA) has compiled this tenth edition of the *Shopping Guide for Caring Consumers* as a part of our international Caring Consumer Project. It's an easy resource to use when shopping for products made by companies that do not test on animals.

The companies listed in this guide have signed PETA's statement of assurance or provided a company policy statement verifying that they:

1) do not conduct animal tests on ingredients or finished products;

2) do not contract with other laboratories to conduct animal tests;

3) will not conduct animal tests in the future;

4) and/or have signed the Corporate Standard of Compassion for Animals (see page 9), which, in addition to verifying the three requirements listed above, also requires companies to obtain statements of assurance from all their suppliers to the effect that no ingredients supplied to them were tested on animals.

WHAT IS THE "CORPORATE STANDARD OF COMPASSION FOR ANIMALS"?

The Coalition for Consumer Information on Cosmetics (CCIC) joins together PETA and seven other animals protection groups that have created a unified policy designed to make it easier for consumers and companies to identify the products that meet ethical standards. The Corporate Standard of Compassion for Animals (CSCA) is that unified policy and PETA is encouraging all companies, including those that have signed PETA's statement of assurance, to adopt the CSCA. For more details about the CCIC or the CSCA, call 1-888-546-CCIC.

BLINDING BUNNIES AND POISONING DOGS — OUTDATED, UNNECESSARY, AND CRUEL

Every year, millions of rabbits, dogs, rats, guinea pigs, and other animals suffer and are killed in painful product tests. Companies claim to use these outdated tests to determine the safety of cosmetics, household, and other consumer products.

However, these tests are widely criticized by scientists as cruel, archaic methods that offer unreliable and often contradictory results. Furthermore, the Food and Drug Administration (FDA) and the Consumer Product Safety Commission do not require the use of animals to test cosmetics and household products.

The notoriously cruel and unnecessary lethal dose tests and the Draize eye irritancy tests, which are still used today, date back to the 1920s. In lethal dose tests, animals are force-fed, injected with, or forced to inhale toxic substances until a designated percentage of them die. In the Draize eye irritancy tests, a substance is typically smeared into the eyes of albino rabbits, usually without anesthesia. The rabbits are restrained, their eyelids held open with clips. The rabbits are forced to endure these conditions for up to 18 days. They suffer discharge, inflammation, ulceration, hemorrhage, and blindness.

Modern technology has enabled hundreds of companies to use non-animal test methods, including human volunteers, in vitro studies, computer models, cloned human skin, tissue cultures, and extensive databases. These sophisticated, reliable, humane alternatives are helping to ensure that cruel product tests on animals will soon be a shameful page in our history books.

9

V IS FOR VEGAN

Skin lotions, shaving cream, toothpaste, and lipstick—many of these cosmetics and personal care products contain slaughter-house byproducts. They may also contain other animal-derived ingredients, including honey, silk and silk byproducts, lanolin, and substances extracted from insects or sea animals.

Many consumers, who refuse to support industries in which animal suffering is inherent, seek out vegan products. PETA lists products as vegan when they are free of any animal products or slaughterhouse byproducts. Vegan products listed in this guide may contain plant- or mineral-based or synthetic ingredients. Companies listed in this guide that are marked with a **V** manufacture only vegan products.

Sometimes labels include ingredients that can be of either vegetable or animal origin, including cetyl alcohol, glycerin, lecithin, mono- and diglycerides, stearic acid, and squaline. When in doubt, contact the manufacturer for details. Please note that most companies on our "don't test" list make some vegan products. Please check with the companies for more information about these products.

For a list of animal ingredients and their alternatives, please contact PETA's Literature Department at 757-622-PETA, extension 418, or visit www.peta-online.org.

LOOK FOR THE NEW LOGO

As part of our involvement with the Coalition for Consumer Information on Cosmetics (CCIC), PETA's Caring Consumer Product Logo has been replaced by CCIC's new product logo. When you see this logo, you can be sure that the product meets non-animal-testing standards set by the Corporate Standard of Compassion for Animals (CSCA).

For more information about product testing or other animal rights issues, please contact:

People for the Ethical Treatment of Animals (PETA)
501 Front St.
Norfolk, VA 23510
757-622-PETA
www.peta-online.org

WHAT TYPES OF COMPANIES ARE ON THE "DON'T TEST" LIST?

The list includes cosmetics, personal care, household cleaning, and office supply product companies only. PETA'S Caring Consumer Project was founded upon the fact that no law requires testing of these types of products, so manufacturers of these products have no excuse for animal testing and should be boycotted in order to pressure them to change to a non-animal-testing policy.

The list does not include companies that manufacture only products that are required by law to be tested on animals (e.g., pharmaceuticals, automotive and garden chemicals, food additives, etc.). While PETA is opposed to all animal testing, our quarrel in this matter is with the regulatory agencies that require animal testing. Nonetheless, it is important to let companies know that it is their responsibility to convince the regulatory agencies that there is a better way to determine product safety.

The "don't test" list may include companies that manufacture both products that are and products that are not required to be tested on animals, but, in order to be listed, each company has stated that it does not conduct any animal tests that are not required by law.

Legend	
V	Vegan. (Companies that manufacture strictly vegan products, i.e., containing no animal products. Companies without this symbol may still offer some vegan products.)
⊞	Company meets Corporate Standard of Compassion for Animals (CSCA).
🖼 🐇	Company using cruelty-free product logo. (All companies listed in the guide are cruelty-free. Many of them have chosen to use a logo to assist consumers.)
MO	Mail order available.

ABBA Products
7400 E. Tierra Buena
Scottsdale, AZ 85260
480-609-6000
800-848-4475
www.styl.com
Products: hair care, dandruff
shampoo, permanents
Availability: boutiques,
specialty stores, distributors,
salons
V 🖾

ABEnterprises
15 Baltimore St., #1A
Staten Island, NY 10308-
2248
718-984-9096
Products: aromatherapy,
bathing supply, deodorant,
shaving supply, soap,
vitamins, herbs
Availability: mail order
MO

Abercrombie & Fitch
4 Limited Pkwy.
Reynoldsburg, OH 43068
614-577-6570
Products: fragrance for men,
toiletries, personal care
Availability: Abercrombie &
Fitch stores, Victoria's Secret
stores

Abkit
207 E. 94th St.
Suite 201
New York, NY 10128
212-860-8358
800-CAMOCARE
Products: skin care, hair
care, toiletries, household
supply
Availability: health food
stores, mail order
MO

Abra Therapeutics
10365 Hwy. 116
Forestville, CA 95436
707-869-0761
800-745-0761
www.abratherapeutics.com
Products: aromatherapy,
hypo-allergenic skin care for
men and women, sun care,
toiletries, bathing supply,
shaving supply, vitamins,
herbs
Availability: health food
stores, boutiques, specialty
stores, spas, mail order
V MO

Advanage Wonder Cleaner
16615 S. Halsted St.
Harvey, IL 60426
708-333-7644
800-323-6444
www.wondercleaner.com
Products: carpet cleaning
supply, laundry detergent,
laundry detergent for fine
washables, oven cleaner
Availability: independent
sales representatives, mail
order
V MO

Ahimsa Natural Care Ltd.
1250 Reid St., Suite 13A
Richmond Hill, ON
L4B 1G3 Canada
905-709-8977
888-424-4672
Products: aromatherapy,
baby care, fragrance for men
and women, hair care,
dandruff shampoo
Availability: health food
stores, cooperatives,
boutiques, specialty stores,
environmentally friendly
stores, mail order
V 🖾 **MO**

Alba Botanica
P.O. Box 40339
Santa Barbara, CA 93140
805-965-0170
800-347-5211
www.albabotanica.com
Products: skin care for men
and women, sun care,
toiletries, bathing supply,
shaving supply, soap
Availability: drugstores,
health food stores,
cooperatives, boutiques,
specialty stores, mail order
MO

**Alexandra Avery Body
Botanicals**
4717 S.E. Belmont
Portland, OR 97215
503-236-5926
800-669-1863
Products: aromatherapy,
lubricants, fragrance for
men and women, skin care,
sun care, toiletries, shaving
supply, soap
Availability: health food
stores, cooperatives,
boutiques, specialty stores,
mail order
MO

**Alexandra de Markoff
(Parlux)**
3725 S.W. 30th Ave.
Ft. Lauderdale, FL 33312
954-316-9008
800-727-5895
Products: cosmetics
Availability: department
stores

Allens Naturally
P.O. Box 514, Dept. M
Farmington, MI 48332-0514
734-453-5410
800-352-8971
www.allensnaturally.com
Products: household supply,
laundry detergent
Availability: health food
stores, cooperatives, mail
order
V ★ MO

Almay (Revlon)
625 Madison Ave.
New York, NY 10022
212-572-5000
Products: cosmetics, ethnic
personal care, hypo-
allergenic skin care for men
and women, sun care,
deodorant
Availability: department
stores, drugstores,
supermarkets

Aloegen Natural Cosmetics
9200 Mason Ave.
Chatsworth, CA 91311
818-882-2951
800-327-2012
Products: skin care
Availability: health food
stores, cooperatives, mail
order
MO

Aloette Cosmetics
1301 Wright's La. E.
West Chester, PA 19380
610-692-0600
800-ALOETTE
Products: cosmetics,
fragrance for men and
women, nail care, skin care
for men and women, sun
care, toiletries, bathing
supply
Availability: independent
sales representatives

Aloe Up
P.O. Box 831
6908 W. Expressway 83
Harlingen, TX 78551
210-428-0081
800-537-2563
Products: hair care,
hypo-allergenic skin care for
men and women, sun care,
toiletries
Availability: drugstores,
health food stores,
supermarkets, boutiques,
specialty stores, mail order
MO

Aloe Vera of America
9660 Dilworth Rd.
Dallas, TX 75243
214-343-5700
Products: aromatherapy,
companion animal care,
cosmetics, dental hygiene,
hair care, household supply,
laundry detergent, skin care,
bathing supply, deodorant,
shaving supply, soap,
vitamins
Availability: independent
sales representatives

Alvin Last
19 Babcock Place
Yonkers, NY 10701
914-376-1000
800-527-8123
Products: cosmetics, dental
hygiene, hair care, dandruff
shampoo, hair color (henna),
skin care for men and
women, toiletries, shaving
supply
Availability: drugstores,
health food stores, mail
order
MO

Amazon Premium Products
P.O. Box 530156
Miami, FL 33153
305-757-1943
800-832-5645
www.amazonpp.com
Products: air freshener,
carpet cleaning supply,
furniture polish
Availability: hardware stores,
mail order
V MO

**American Formulating &
Manufacturing**
350 W. Ash St., Suite 700
San Diego, CA 92101
619-239-0321
800-239-0321
www.afmsafecoat.com
Products: hair care,
household supply, carpet
cleaning supply, paint, stain,
cleaners, floor finishes
Availability: cooperatives,
specialty stores, mail order
V MO

American International
2220 Gaspar Ave.
Los Angeles, CA 90040
213-728-2999
Products: skin care, toiletries
Availability: discount
department stores,
drugstores, health food
stores, supermarkets,
boutiques, specialty stores,
beauty supply stores

American Safety Razor
P.O. Box 500
Staunton, VA 24402
540-248-8000
800-445-9284
Products: aromatherapy,
razors, blades, toiletries,
bathing supply, shaving
supply, soap, Personna,
Flicker, Burma Shave, Gem,
Bump Fighter
Availability: department
stores, discount department
stores, drugstores, health
food stores, supermarkets,
boutiques, specialty stores,
mail order
🖼 MO

**America's Finest Products
Corporation**
1639 Ninth St.
Santa Monica, CA 90404
310-450-6555
800-482-6555
Products: household supply,
laundry soil-stain remover,
cool-water wash for
delicates, multipurpose
cleaner, concrete cleaner,
elbow grease, liquid cleaner,
water softener
Availability: drugstores,
supermarkets, mail order
V MO

**Amitée Cosmetics
(Advanced Research Labs)**
151 Kalmus Dr., Suite H3
Costa Mesa, CA 92626
714-556-1028
800-966-6960
Products: hair care
Availability: drugstores,
supermarkets, beauty supply
stores

Amoresse Laboratories
4121 Buchanan St.
Riverside, CA 92503
800-258-7931
Products: nail care
Availability: salons

Amway Corporation
7575 E. Fulton Rd.
Ada, MI 49355-0001
616-787-4278
www.amway.com
Products: cosmetics, dental
hygiene, fragrance, hair
care, dandruff shampoo, car
care, carpet cleaning supply,
furniture polish, laundry
detergent, oven cleaner,
insect repellant, skin care,
sun care
Availability: independent
sales representatives, mail
order
MO

The Ananda Collection
14618 Tyler Foote Rd.
Nevada City, CA 95959
916-478-7575
800-537-8766
tacjoy@nccn.net
Products: fragrance for men
and women, household
supply, air freshener,
massage oil
Availability: drugstores,
health food stores,
cooperatives, boutiques,
specialty stores, mail order
V MO

Ancient Formulas
638 W. 33rd St. N.
Wichita, KS 67204
316-838-5600
800-543-3026
Products: hypo-allergenic/
acne skin care for men and
women, herbal supplements
for blood pressure,
respiratory health, sleeping
aid, carbohydrate balance,
irregularity, prostate health
Availability: drugstores,
health food stores,
cooperatives, mail order,
physicians
MO

**Andrea International
Industries**
2220 Gaspar Ave.
Los Angeles, CA 90040
213-728-2999
Products: nail care, skin care
for women
Availability: discount
department stores,
drugstores, supermarkets,
boutiques, specialty stores,
mass retailers

The Apothecary Shoppe
P.O. Box 57
Lake Oswego, OR 97034
503-635-6652
800-487-8839
www.herbed.com
Products: aromatherapy,
herbs, homeobotanicals,
flower essences, iridology
supply
Availability: mail order, Web
site
MO

Aramis (Estée Lauder)
767 Fifth Ave.
New York, NY 10153
212-572-3700
Products: fragrance for men
and women, hair care,
razors, skin care for men,
sun care, toiletries, bathing
supply, deodorant, shaving
supply, soap
Availability: department
stores, specialty stores

15

Arbonne International
P.O. Box 2488
Laguna Hills, CA 92654
949-770-2610
800-ARBONNE
www.arbonneinternational.com
Products: cosmetics,
fragrance for women, hair
care, hypo-allergenic skin
care for men and women,
sun care, bathing supply,
shaving supply, vitamins,
herbs
Availability: independent
sales representatives, mail
order
MO

Ardell International
2220 Gaspar Ave.
Los Angeles, CA 90040
213-728-2999
Products: nail care, skin care
for women
Availability: discount
department stores,
drugstores, supermarkets,
boutiques, specialty stores,
mass retailers

Arizona Natural Resources
2525 E. Beardsley Rd.
Phoenix, AZ 85024
602-569-6900
Products: cosmetics, baby
care, hair care, hypo-
allergenic skin care for men
and women, sun care,
toiletries
Availability: discount
department stores, drug-
stores, health food stores,
supermarkets, boutiques,
distributors, warehouse
clubs, mail order
MO

Aromaland
1326 Rufina Cir.
Santa Fe, NM 87505
505-438-0402
800-933-5267
www.buyaromatherapy.com
Products: aromatherapy,
fragrance for men and
women, air freshener, insect
repellant, bathing supply
Availability: health food
stores, cooperatives,
boutiques, specialty stores,
New Age bookstores, mail
order, Web site
MO

Aroma Vera
5901 Rodeo Rd.
Los Angeles, CA 90016-4312
310-280-0407
800-669-9514
www.aromavera.com
Products: aromatherapy,
fragrance for men and
women, hair care, air
freshener, skin care for men
and women, toiletries,
bathing supply, soap, gift
items
Availability: health food
stores, Aroma Vera stores,
boutiques, specialty stores,
salons, spas, mail order
MO

Astonish Industries Inc.
Commerce Lane Business Park
423 Commerce La., Unit 2
West Berlin, NJ 08091
609-753-7078
800-530-5385
Products: household supply,
carpet cleaning supply, oven
cleaner, dish detergent
Availability: specialty stores,
QVC, mail order

**Atmosa Brand
Aromatherapy Products**
1420 Fifth Ave., 22nd Fl.
Suite 2200
Seattle, WA 98101-2378
206-521-5986
206-621-6567
Products: aromatherapy,
home fragrance
Availability: department
stores, boutiques, specialty
stores

Aubrey Organics
4419 N. Manhattan Ave.
Tampa, FL 33614
813-877-4186
800-AUBREYH
www.aubrey-organics.com
Products: baby care,
companion animal care,
cosmetics, fragrance for men
and women, hair care, hair
color, household supply,
insect repellant, skin care,
sun care, bathing supply,
deodorant, shaving supply
Availability: health food
stores, mail order
MO

Aunt Bee's Skin Care
P.O. Box 2678
Rancho de Taos, NM 87577
505-737-0522
Products: skin care, personal
care, lip balm
Availability: drugstores, health
food stores, supermarkets,
mail order
MO

Aura Cacia
P.O. Box 299
Norway, IA 52318
800-437-3301
Products: aromatherapy,
baby care, fragrance for men
and women, skin care,
toiletries, bathing supply, soap
Availability: discount
department stores,
drugstores, health food
stores, cooperatives,
boutiques, specialty stores,
mail order
V MO

Auroma International
P.O. Box 1008
Silver Lake, WI 53170
414-889-8501
Products: dental hygiene,
fragrance for men and
women, household supply,
air freshener, toiletries,
incense
Availability: drugstores, health
food stores, supermarkets,
cooperatives, mail order
V MO

**Auromère Ayurvedic
Imports**
2621 W. Highway 12
Lodi, CA 95242
209-339-3710
800-735-4691
Products: dental hygiene,
skin care for men and
women, toiletries, bathing
supply, soap, vitamins,
herbs, ayurvedic, incense,
massage oil
Availability: health food
stores, cooperatives, New
Age stores, mail order
V ★ ☆ MO

**The Australasian College of
Herbal Studies**
P.O. Box 57
Lake Oswego, OR 97034
503-635-6652
800-487-8839
www.herbed.com
Products: aromatherapy,
herbs, correspondence
courses in natural healing
Availability: mail order, Web site
MO

Autumn-Harp
61 Pine St.
Bristol, VT 04551
802-453-4807
Products: aromatherapy, baby
care, cosmetics, sun care,
personal care, nonprescription
therapy
Availability: department stores,
drugstores, health food stores,
supermarkets, cooperatives,
mail order
★ MO

Avalon Organic Botanicals
P.O. Box 750428
Petaluma, CA 94975-0428
707-769-5120
www.avalonproducts.net
Products: hair care,
hypo-allergenic skin care for
men and women, toiletries,
bathing supply, deodorant,
soap
Availability: health food
stores, boutiques, specialty
stores, mail order
MO

Aveda Corporation
4000 Pheasant Ridge Dr.
Blaine, MN 55449
612-783-4000
800-328-0849
www.aveda.com
Products: cosmetics, hair
care, skin care, Pure-fume
(R), lifestyle items, ethnic
personal care
Availability: salons, spas,
environmentally friendly
stores, health care facilities,
educational institutions

Avigal Henna
45-49 Davis St.
Long Island City, NY 11101
800-722-1011
Products: henna hair color
Availability: health food
stores, specialty stores, salons
V

Avon
1251 Avenue of the
Americas
New York, NY 10020
212-546-6015
800-858-8000
www.avon.com
Products: cosmetics, ethnic
personal care, fragrance for
men and women, hair care,
dandruff shampoo, nail care,
hypo-allergenic skin care for
men and women, sun care,
toiletries, Skin So Soft insect
repellant
Availability: distributors,
mail order
MO

Ayurherbal Corporation
1100 Lotus Dr.
Silver Lake, WI 53170
414-889-8569
Products: dental hygiene,
fragrance for men and
women, household supply,
air freshener, toiletries,
incense
Availability: drugstores,
health food stores,
cooperatives, boutiques,
specialty stores, mail order
V MO

Ayurveda Holistic Center
82A Bayville Ave.
Bayville, NY 11709
516-628-8200
www.ayurvedahc.com
Products: ayurvedic herbs
for humans and companion
animals
Availability: health food
stores, Ayurveda Holistic
Center stores
V

Bare Escentuals
600 Townsend St., Suite 329-E
San Francisco, CA 94103
415-487-3400
800-227-3990
Products: aromatherapy,
cosmetics, fragrance, hair
care, nail care, hypo-
allergenic skin care,
toiletries, bathing supply,
deodorant, shaving
supply, soap
Availability: department
stores, Bare Escentuals
stores, boutiques, specialty
stores, mail order
MO

Basically Natural
109 E. G St.
Brunswick, MD 21716
301-834-7923
800-352-7099
Products: aromatherapy,
baby care, companion
animal care, cosmetics,
dental hygiene, hair care,
car care, household supply,
air freshener, bleach,
laundry detergent, oven
cleaner, insect repellant,
hypo-allergenic skin care,
sun care, toiletries
Availability: mail order
V MO

Basic Elements Hair Care

505 S. Beverly Dr.
Suite 1292
Beverly Hills, CA 90212
800-947-5522
Products: hair care, skin care
for men and women
Availability: salons, mail order
V MO

Basis (Beiersdorf)
BDF Plaza
360 Martin Luther King Dr.
Norwalk, CT 06856-5529
203-853-8008
Products: soap
Availability: drugstores,
supermarkets

Bath & Body Works
7 Limited Pkwy. E.
Reynoldsburg, OH 43068
614-856-6585
800-395-1001
Products: aromatherapy,
baby care, cosmetics,
fragrance, hair care, air
freshener, insect repellant, nail
care, hypo-allergenic skin
care, sun care, bathing supply,
deodorant, shaving supply,
soap
Availability: Bath & Body
Works stores

Bath Island
469 Amsterdam Ave.
New York, NY 10024
212-787-9415
www.bathisland.com
Products: aromatherapy,
baby care, dental hygiene,
toothbrushes, fragrance, hair
care, dandruff shampoo,
household supply, air
freshener, nail care, razors,
skin care, sun care, bathing
supply, deodorant, soap
Availability: Bath Island
store, mail order
MO

Baudelaire
166 Emerald St.
Keene, NH 03431
603-352-9234
800-327-2324
www.baudelairesoaps.com
Products: aromatherapy,
baby care, fragrance for men
and women, skin care,
toiletries, bathing supply,
shaving supply, soap
Availability: health food
stores, boutiques, specialty
stores, mail order
★ MO

BeautiControl Cosmetics
2121 Midway Rd.
Carrollton, TX 75006
972-458-0601
www.beauticontrol.com
Products: cosmetics,
fragrance for men and
women, nail care, sun care,
hypo-allergenic skin care
Availability: distributors

Beauty Naturally
P.O. Box 4905
850 Stanton Rd.
Burlingame, CA 94010
650-697-1845
800-432-4323
Products: hair care, dandruff
shampoo, hair color,
permanents, hypo-allergenic
skin care for men and
women, deodorant
Availability: health food
stores, mail order
MO

**Beauty Without Cruelty
Cosmetics**
P.O. Box 750428
Petaluma, CA 94975-0428
707-769-5120
Products: aromatherapy,
cosmetics, hair care, nail
care, hypo-allergenic skin
care for men and women,
sun care, toiletries, bathing
supply, soap
Availability: health food
stores, boutiques, specialty
stores, mail order
V MO

Beehive Botanicals
16297 W. Nursery Rd.
Hayward, WI 54843
715-634-4274
800-233-4483
www.beehive-botanicals.com
Products: dental hygiene,
hair care, skin care for
women, toiletries, bathing
supply, soap, herbs
Availability: health food
stores, mail order
MO

Beiersdorf
BDF Plaza
360 Martin Luther King Dr.
Norwalk, CT 06856-5529
203-853-8008
Products: skin care, Nivea,
Eucerin, Basis soap, La Prairie
Availability: drugstores,
supermarkets

Bella's Secret Garden
6059 Sikorsky St.
Ventura, CA 93003
805-639-5020
800-962-6867
Products: baby care,
fragrance for women, hair
care, household supply, air
freshener, hypo-allergenic
skin care for men and
women, toiletries
Availability: department
stores, drugstores, boutiques,
small gift stores

Belle Star
23151 Alcalde, #A-1
Laguna Hills, CA 92653
714-768-7006
800-442-STAR
Products: fragrance for men
and women, toiletries, incense,
aromatherapy
Availability: Belle Star store,
boutiques, specialty stores,
craft shows, mail order

Berol (Sanford)
2711 Washington Blvd.
Bellwood, IL 60104
708-547-5525
800-438-3703
www.sanfordcorp.com
Products: office supply, ink,
writing instruments
Availability: department
stores, drugstores, supermarkets, office supply stores,
mail order
MO

Better Botanicals
335 Victory Dr.
Herndon, VA 20170
202-625-6815
888-BB-HERBS
www.betterbotanicals.com
Products: aromatherapy,
baby care, ayurvedic hair
care, ayurvedic skin care for
men and women, bathing
supply, soap
Availability: department
stores, health food stores,
cooperatives, boutiques,
specialty stores, independent
sales representatives, holistic
institutions, mail order
MO

P.O. Box 600476
San Diego, CA 92160
619-283-0880
800-833-0889
Products: cold wax natural
hair remover
Availability: health food
stores, beauty supply stores,
salons, mail order
MO

BioFilm
3121 Scott St.
Vista, CA 92083
619-727-9030
800-848-5900
Products: Astroglide
personal lubricant
Availability: drugstores
V

Legend
V Vegan (products
contain no animal
ingredients)
★ Company meets
CSCA
Company uses
Caring Consumer
product logo
MO Mail order
available

Biogime
25602 I-45 N.
Suite 106
Spring, TX 77386
281-298-2607
800-338-8784
Products: cosmetics, hypo-
allergenic skin care for men
and women, sun care,
theatrical makeup, bathing
supply, lotions
Availability: independent sales
representatives, mail order
V MO

Biokosma (Caswell-Massey)
100 Enterprise Place
Dover, DE 19904
800-326-0500
Products: toiletries
Availability: specialty stores,
mail order
MO

Bio Pac
584 Pinto Ct.
Incline Village, NV 89451
800-225-2855
www.bio-pac.com
Products: nonchlorine bleach,
laundry detergent, soap
Availability: health food
stores, cooperatives,
independent sales representatives, mail order
V ★ MO

Bio-Tec Cosmetics
92 Sherwood Ave.
Toronto, ON M4P 2A7
Canada
800-667-2524
Products: cosmetics, hair
care, permanents, hair color,
skin care for men and
women, toiletries
Availability: hair care in
beauty salons, bath and skin
care in retail outlets

Biotone
4757 Old Cliffs Rd.
San Diego, CA 92120
619-582-0027
Products: aromatherapy,
massage creams, oil and
lotion for massage therapists,
hypo-allergenic skin care
Availability: boutiques,
specialty stores, independent
sales representatives, direct
to massage therapists, mail
order
MO

Bobbi Brown (Estée Lauder)
767 Fifth Ave.
New York, NY 10153
212-572-4200
Products: cosmetics, ethnic
personal care
Availability: department
stores

Bo-Chem Company (Neway)
42 Doaks La.
Marblehead, MA 01945
617-631-9400
Products: household supply
Availability: distributors,
mail order
MO

Body Encounters
604 Manor Rd.
Cinnamonson, NJ 08077
800-839-2639
www.bodyencounters.com
Products: aromatherapy, skin
care for men and women,
sun care, toiletries, bathing
supply, soap, shaving supply
Availability: mail order, Web
site
MO

Bodyography
1641 16th St.
Santa Monica, CA 90404
310-399-2886
800-642-2639
Products: cosmetics
Availability: beauty supply
stores, salons

The Body Shop
5036 One World Way
Wake Forest, NC 27587
919-554-4900
800-541-2535
www.the-body-shop.com
Products: aromatherapy,
baby care, cosmetics, dental
hygiene, toothbrushes,
fragrance, hair care, hair
color, nail care, razors, skin
care, sun care, toiletries,
bathing supply, deodorant,
shaving supply, soap
Availability: The Body Shop
stores, mail order
★ MO

Body Time
1101 Eighth St., Suite 100
Berkeley, CA 94710
510-524-0216
888-649-2639
www.bodytime.com
Products: aromatherapy,
baby care, hair care, air
freshener, skin care, sun
care, toiletries, bathing
supply, shaving supply, soap,
essential oil, massage oil
and lotion, botanicals
Availability: Body Time
stores, mail order
MO

BRONZO SENSUALÉ
FOR THE SENSUOUS LOOK THAT GETS YOU THAT SECOND GLANCE.

For more information, visit our Web site: www.bronzosensuale.com
or contact **BRONZO SENSUALÉ**: 1020 Stillwater Dr., Miami Beach, FL 33141

(800) 991-2226 • (305) 867-1744

Bon Ami/Faultless Starch
510 Walnut St.
Kansas City, MO 64106-1209
816-842-1230
Products: household supply
Availability: drugstores,
health food stores,
supermarkets, cooperatives

Bonne Bell
18519 Detroit Ave.
Georgetown Row
Lakewood, OH 44107
216-221-0800
www.bonnebell.com
Products: Cosmetics, nail
care, skin care for women,
sun care, toiletries, bathing
supply, soap
Availability: discount
department stores, drug-
stores, supermarkets

Börlind of Germany
P.O. Box 130
New London, NH 03257
603-526-2076
800-447-7024
Products: aromatherapy,
cosmetics, hair care,
toiletries
Availability: health food
stores, boutiques, specialty
stores, salons, spas

Botan Corporation
2620 Drayton Dr.
Louisville, KY 40205-2332
502-772-0800
800-448-0800
Products: hypo-allergenic skin
care for men and women,
toiletries, shaving supply
Availability: department
stores, drugstores, health
food stores, specialty stores,
distributors, environmentally
friendly bath stores, mail
order
V MO

21

Botanics Skin Care
P.O. Box 384
Ukiah, CA 95482
707-462-6141
800-800-6141
Products: hair care, hypo-allergenic skin care, sun care
Availability: department stores, health food stores, cooperatives, boutiques, specialty stores, mail order
V MO

Brocato International
1 Main St., Suite 501
Minneapolis, MN 55414
800-243-0275
Products: hair care, dandruff shampoo, permanents
Availability: boutiques, specialty stores, salons
V

Bronzo Sensualé
1020 Stillwater Dr.
Miami Beach, FL 33141
305-867-1744
800-991-2226
www.bronzosensuale.com
Products: aromatherapy, baby care, hypo-allergenic skin care for men and women, sun care
Availability: drugstores, health food stores, boutiques, specialty stores, spas, resorts, mail order
V ★ MO

Brookside Soap Company
P.O. Box 55638
Seattle, WA 98155
206-742-2265
Products: companion animal care, soap
Availability: health food stores, supermarkets in Washington state, mail order
V MO

Bug Off
197 N. Willard St.
Burlington, VT 05401
802-865-6290
Products: herbal insect repellent for home, people, and companion animals
Availability: health food stores, cooperatives, sporting goods stores, veterinarians, environmentally friendly stores, mail order
V MO

Caeran, Inc.
280 King George Rd.
Brantford, ON N3R 5L6
Canada
519-751-0513
800-563-2974
Products: baby care, companion animal care, hair care, dandruff shampoo, household supply, car care, carpet cleaning supply, laundry detergent, hypo-allergenic skin care, sun care, toiletries, bathing supply, deodorant, soap, vitamins, herbs
Availability: health food stores, boutiques, specialty stores, independent sales representatives, mail order
MO

California SunCare
10877 Wilshire Blvd., 12th Fl.
Los Angeles, CA 90024
800-SUN-CARE
Products: skin care for men and women, self-tanning products
Availability: salons

CamoCare Camomile Skin Care Products
207 E. 94th St., Suite 201
New York, NY 10128
212-860-8358
800-CAMOCARE
Products: hair care, skin care
Availability: health food stores, mail order
MO

Candy Kisses Natural Lip Balm
16 E. 40th St., 12th Fl.
New York, NY 10016
212-951-3035
www.candykisses.com
Products: cosmetics
Availability: discount department stores, drugstores, supermarkets, mail order
V ★ MO

Carina Supply
464 Granville St.
Vancouver, BC V6C 1V4
Canada
604-687-3617
Products: companion animal care, hair care, dandruff shampoo, hair color, permanents, hypo-allergenic skin care for men and women
Availability: Carina Supply stores, salons, companion animal supply stores, groomers, veterinarians, mail order
MO

Carlson Laboratories
15 College Dr.
Arlington Heights, IL 60004
847-255-1600
800-323-4141
Products: hair care, skin care, toiletries, vitamins, personal care
Availability: health food stores

Carma Laboratories
5801 W. Airways Ave.
Franklin, WI 53132
414-421-7707
Products: personal care,
Carmex lip balm/cold sore
medicine, nonprescription
therapy
Availability: discount
department stores,
drugstores, health food
stores, supermarkets,
cooperatives, mail order
MO

Caswell-Massey
121 Fieldcrest Ave.
Edison, NJ 08818
201-225-2181
800-326-0500
www.caswellmasseyltd.com
Products: aromatherapy,
baby care, dental hygiene,
toothbrushes, fragrance, hair
care, skin care, toiletries,
bathing supply, deodorant,
shaving supply, soap
Availability: department
stores, discount department
stores, drugstores, health
food stores, Caswell-Massey
stores, boutiques, specialty
stores, mail order
MO

Celestial Body (Face Food Shoppe)
21298 Pleasant Hill Rd.
Boonville, MO 65233
660-882-6858
800-882-6858
Products: aromatherapy,
feminine hygiene, hypo-
allergenic skin care for men
and women, toiletries,
bathing supply, shaving
supply, soap
Availability: health food
stores, cooperatives,
boutiques, specialty stores,
independent sales representatives, mail order
MO

Chanel
9 W. 57th St.
New York, NY 10019
212-688-5055
Products: cosmetics,
fragrance for men and
women, nail care, skin care
for men and women, sun
care, toiletries, deodorant,
soap
Availability: department
stores, Chanel stores

Chatoyant Pearl Cosmetics
P.O. Box 526
Port Townsend, WA 98368
206-385-4825
Products: skin care, toiletries
Availability: health food
stores

Christian Dior Perfumes
9 W. 57th St.
New York, NY 10019
212-759-1840
Products: cosmetics,
fragrance for men and
women, nail care, skin care,
toiletries
Availability: department
stores, boutiques, specialty
stores

Christine Valmy
285 Change Bridge Rd.
Pine Brook, NJ 07058
201-575-1050
800-526-5057
Products: cosmetics,
hypo-allergenic skin care for
men and women, sun care,
toiletries, shaving supply
Availability: salons, J.C.
Penney stores, spas, mail
order
MO

Chuckles (Farmavita)
P.O. Box 5126
Manchester, NH 03109
603-669-4228
800-221-3496
Products: hair care, hair
color, permanents
Availability: salons

CiCi Cosmetics
215 N. Eucalyptus Ave.
Inglewood, CA 90301
310-680-9696
800-869-1224
Products: cosmetics
Availability: discount
department stores,
drugstores, boutiques,
specialty stores, beauty and
theatrical supply stores, mail
order
MO

Cinema Secrets, Inc.
4400 Riverside Dr.
Burbank, CA 91505
818-846-0579
Products: cosmetics,
theatrical makeup
Availability: Cinema
Secrets stores, beauty supply
stores, salons, costume/
novelty stores, mail order
V MO

Citius USA
120 Interstate N. Pkwy. E.
Suite 106
Atlanta, GA 30339
770-953-3663
800-343-9099
Products: office supply,
environmentally safe
correction fluid
Availability: office supply
stores, independent sales
representatives, Sanford
Corporation
V

Citré Shine (Advanced Research Labs)
151 Kalmus Dr., Suite H3
Costa Mesa, CA 92626
714-556-1028
800-966-6960
Products: ethnic personal care, hair care, dandruff shampoo, skin care for men and women
Availability: drugstores, supermarkets, beauty supply stores, General Nutrition Centers

Clarins of Paris
135 E. 57th St.
New York, NY 10022
212-980-1800
Products: cosmetics, fragrance for women, nail care, hypo-allergenic skin care, sun care, toiletries
Availability: department stores, boutiques, specialty stores

Clear Conscience
P.O. Box 17855
Arlington, VA 22216-1785
703-527-7566
800-595-9592
www.clearconscience.com
Products: contact lens solutions
Availability: health food stores, supermarkets, cooperatives, PETA catalog, mail order, Web site
V MO

Clearly Natural Products
1340 N. McDowell Blvd.
Petaluma, CA 94954
707-762-5815
www.clearlynaturalsoaps.com
Products: toiletries, vegetable glycerin soap, liquid glycerin soap
Availability: drugstores, health food stores, supermarkets, Web site
V ★ ▨

Clear Vue Products
P.O. Box 567
417 Canal St.
Lawrence, MA 01842
508-683-7151
508-794-3100
Products: household supply, window cleaner
Availability: supermarkets in New England, mail order
V MO

Legend	
V	Vegan (products contain no animal ingredients)
★	Company meets CSCA
▨	Company uses Caring Consumer product logo
MO	Mail order available

24

Clientele
14101 N.W. Fourth St.
Sunrise, FL 33325
954-845-9500
800-327-4660
Products: cosmetics,
fragrance for men and
women, hair care,
hypo-allergenic skin care for
men and women, sun care,
theatrical makeup, toiletries,
vitamins
Availability: department
stores, boutiques, specialty
stores, mail order

**Clinique Laboratories (Estée
Lauder)**
767 Fifth Ave.
New York, NY 10153
212-572-3800
Products: cosmetics, ethnic
personal care, fragrance,
hair care, nail care,
allergy-tested skin care, sun
care, toiletries, bathing
supply, deodorant, shaving
supply, soap
Availability: department
stores, specialty stores

Colorations
2875 Berkeley Lake Rd.
Duluth, GA 30096
770-417-1501
Products: children's art and
school supply
Availability: school supply,
toy, and gift stores

Color Me Beautiful
14000 Thunderbolt Place
Suite E
Chantilly, VA 20151
703-471-6400
800-533-5503
Products: cosmetics,
fragrance, skin care for men
and women, sun care
Availability: department
stores, drugstores, boutiques,
specialty stores, independent
sales representatives, mail
order

Color My Image, Inc.
5025B Backlick Rd.
Annandale, VA 22003
703-354-9797
Products: cosmetics, nail
care, hypo-allergenic skin
care, sun care, theatrical
makeup, toiletries, bathing
supply, camouflage makeup
Availability: Color My Image
stores, mail order

**Columbia Cosmetics
Manufacturing**
1661 Timothy Dr.
San Leandro, CA 94577
510-562-5900
800-824-3328
Products: aromatherapy,
cosmetics, fragrance, hair
care, nail care, skin care,
sun care, soap
Availability: boutiques,
specialty stores, distributors,
mail order

Common Scents
128 Main St.
Port Jefferson, NY 11777
516-473-6370
Products: aromatherapy,
fragrance for men and
women, bathing supply,
soap
Availability: Common Scents
stores, mail order

Compar, Inc.
70 E. 55th St.
New York, NY 10022
212-980-9620
Products: fragrance for men
and women, toiletries
Availability: department
stores

**The Compassionate
Consumer**
P.O. Box 27
Jericho, NY 11753
718-359-3983
800-733-4134
Products: cosmetics,
household supply,
toiletries, leather
substitutes
Availability: mail order

Compassionate Cosmetics
P.O. Box 3534
Glendale, CA 91201
Products: cosmetics,
toiletries, perfume
Availability: mail order

Compassion Matters
2 E. Fourth St.
Jamestown, NY 14701
716-664-7023
800-422-6330
Products: aromatherapy,
baby care, companion
animal care, cosmetics,
dental hygiene,
toothbrushes, fragrance, hair
care, dandruff shampoo,
household supply, laundry
detergent, insect repellant,
razors, skin care, sun care
Availability: Compassion
Matters store, mail order
MO

Conair
1 Cummings Point Rd.
Stamford, CT 06904
203-351-9000
800-7-CONAIR
www.conair.com
Products: Jheri Redding hair
care, hair color, permanents,
toiletries, Conair hair care
styling tools
Availability: discount
department stores,
drugstores, supermarkets,
beauty supply stores, mail
order
MO

**Concept Now Cosmetics
(CNC)**
P.O. Box 3208
Santa Fe Springs, CA 90670
310-903-1450
800-CNC-1215
Products: cosmetics, skin
care for men and women,
sun care
Availability: distributors,
mail order
MO

Cosmair (L'Oréal)
575 Fifth Ave.
New York, NY 10017
212-818-1500
Products: cosmetics,
fragrance for men and
women, hair color, nail care
Availability: department
stores, drugstores,
supermarkets, boutiques,
specialty stores

Cosmyl, Inc.
1 Cosmyl Place, Corporate
Ridge Industrial Park
Columbus, GA 31907
706-569-6100
800-262-4401
Products: cosmetics,
fragrance for women, nail
care, skin care for men and
women, toiletries
Availability: department
stores, boutiques, specialty
stores, J.C. Penney stores,
Sears store

Cot 'n Wash
502 The Times Bldg.
Ardmore, PA 19003
610-896-4373
800-355-WASH
Products: household supply,
soap for fine washables
Availability: department
stores, health food stores,
cooperatives, boutiques,
specialty stores,
mail order
V MO

Country Comfort
P.O. Box 406
Fawnskin, CA 92333
909-866-3678
800-462-6617
Products: baby care, healing
salve, lip balm
Availability: health food
stores, mail order
⊠ MO

Country Save
3410 Smith Ave.
Everett, WA 98201
206-258-1171
Products: household supply,
chlorine-free bleach,
laundry detergent, dish
detergent
Availability: health food
stores, supermarkets,
cooperatives, available in
Canada at select stores
V

Countryside Fragrances
Pacific First Centre, 22nd Fl.
1420 Fifth Ave.
Seattle, WA 98101-2378
814-587-6331
800-447-8901
Products: potpourri,
wardrobe sachets, essential
oil, aromatherapy oil,
simmering potpourri,
mulling spices for cider and
wine
Availability: department
stores, boutiques, wholesale
to other companies,
V

Crabtree & Evelyn Ltd.
Peake Brook Rd.
Box 167
Woodstock, CT 06281
203-928-2761
800-624-5211
www.crabtree-evelyn-usa.com
Products: baby care,
toothbrushes, fragrance for
men and women, air
freshener, razors, toiletries,
shaving supply
Availability: Crabtree &
Evelyn stores, department
stores, boutiques, specialty
stores

Crème de la Terre
30 Cook Rd.
Stamford, CT 06902
203-324-4300
800-260-0700
Products: hypo-allergenic
skin care for men and
women, sun care, toiletries
Availability: health food
stores, boutiques, specialty
stores, mail order
MO

Crown Royale Ltd.
P.O. Box 5238
99 Broad St.
Phillipsburg, NJ 08865
908-859-6488
800-992-5400
Products: companion animal
care, fragrance for men and
women, household supply,
carpet cleaning supply,
toiletries, shaving supply
Availability: grooming
shops, distributors, mail
order
V MO

CYA Products, Inc.
6671 W. Indiantown Rd.
Suite 56-191
Jupiter, FL 33458
561-744-2998
www.adzorbstar.com
Products: air freshener
Availability: health food
stores, boutiques, specialty
stores, companion animal
supply stores, distributors,
mail order
V MO

Dallas Manufacturing Co.
4215 McEwen Rd.
Dallas, TX 75244
214-716-4200
800-256-8669
Products: companion animal
care
Availability: discount
department stores,
supermarkets, companion
animal supply stores,
wholesale, mail order
MO

Decleor USA
18 E. 48th St., 21st Fl.
New York, NY 10017
212-838-1771
800-722-2219
Products: cosmetics,
fragrance for men and
women, hair care, dandruff
shampoo, nail care, hypo-
allergenic skin care for men
and women, sun care,
toiletries, shaving supply
Availability: department
stores, boutiques, specialty
stores, skin care salons,
spas, Decleor stores

**Deodorant Stones of
America**
9420 E. Doubletree Ranch Rd.
Suite C-101
Scottsdale, AZ 85258
602-451-4981
800-279-9318
Products: deodorant stones
Availability: drugstores,
health food stores,
supermarkets, mail order
V ⬀ MO

Derma-E Skin & Hair Care
9400 Lurline Ave., Suite C-1
Chatsworth, CA 91311
818-718-1420
800-521-3342
www.derma-e.com
Products: aromatherapy, hair
care, dandruff shampoo,
hypo-allergenic skin care for
men and women, sun care,
toiletries, bathing supply,
soap
Availability: health food
stores, beauty supply stores,
mail order
MO

Dermalogica
1001 Knox St.
Torrance, CA 90502
310-352-4784
800-345-2761
www.dermalogica.com
Products: hypo-allergenic
skin care for men and
women, sun care, bathing
supply, vitamins, herbs
Availability: boutiques,
specialty stores, skin care
salons, physicians, spas

**Dermatologic Cosmetic
Laboratories**
20 Commerce St.
East Haven, CT 06512
203-467-1570
800-552-5060
Products: hair care, dandruff
shampoo, skin care for men
and women, sun care,
toiletries, bathing supply,
soap
Availability: physicians,
aestheticians

Desert Essence
9700 Topanga Canyon Blvd.
Chatsworth, CA 91311
818-734-1735
800-848-7331
Products: aromatherapy, dental hygiene, hair care, skin care, toiletries, deodorant, soap
Availability: health food stores, boutiques, specialty stores

DeSoto
900 E. Washington St.
P.O. Box 609
Joliet, IL 60434
815-727-4931
800-544-2814
Products: private-label household supply
Availability: supermarkets, drugstores

Diamond Brands
1660 S. Highway 100
Suite 590
Minneapolis, MN 55416
612-541-1500
Products: cosmetics, nail care, La Salle "10" nail treatments
Availability: discount department stores, drugstores, supermarkets

Donna Karan (Estée Lauder)
767 Fifth Ave.
New York, NY 10153
212-572-4200
Products: fragrance
Availability: department stores

Dr. A.C. Daniels, Inc.
109 Worcester Rd.
Webster, MA 01570
508-943-5563
800-547-3760
www.drdaniels.com
Products: companion animal care
Availability: companion animal supply stores, mail order

Dr. Bronner's Magic Soaps
P.O. Box 28
Escondido, CA 92033-0028
760-738-7474
Products: baby care, companion animal care, hair care, toiletries, castille soaps, all-purpose cleaner
Availability: health food stores, cooperatives, sporting goods stores

Dr. Goodpet
P.O. Box 4547
Inglewood, CA 90309
310-672-3269
800-222-9932
www.goodpet.com
Products: companion animal care, vitamins
Availability: drugstores, health food stores, companion animal supply stores, mail order,
⭐ MO

Dr. Hauschka Skin Care
59C North St.
Hatfield, MA 01038
413-247-9907
800-247-9907
Products: cosmetics, skin care for men and women, sun care, toiletries, bathing supply, deodorant
Availability: health food stores, boutiques, specialty stores

D.R.P.C. (AmerAgain)
567-1 S. Leonard St.
Waterbury, CT 06708
203-755-3123
Products: environmentally friendly, recycled office supply
Availability: office supply stores, environmentally friendly stores
V

Dr. Singha's Natural Therapeutics
2500 Side Cove
Austin, TX 78704
512-444-2862
www.drsingha.com
Products: aromatherapy, air freshener, bathing supply
Availability: health food stores, boutiques, specialty stores, spas, mail order
V MO

Earth Friendly Products
855 Lively Blvd.
P.O. Box 607
Wood Dale, IL 60191-2688
630-595-1933
800-335-3267
www.ecos.com
Products: hair care, household supply, air freshener, furniture polish, laundry detergent, personal care
Availability: drugstores, health food stores, supermarkets, cooperatives, mail order
▨ MO

Dr. Goodpet
Naturally... it's the best.

The Dr. Goodpet family of homeopathic medicines

- Natural Remedies for dogs and cats
- No side effects
- Flea Relief
- Scratch Free
- Calm Stress
- Ear Relief
- Diar-Relief
- Good Breath
- Arthritis Relief
- Eye-C

Dr. Goodpet
P.O. Box 4547, Inglewood, CA 90309
(800) 222-9932 Fax (310) 672-4287

Visit our website: www.goodpet.com

Earthly Matters
2950 St. Augustine Rd.
Jacksonville, FL 32207
904-398-1458
800-398-7503
Products: household supply,
carpet cleaning supply, air
freshener, furniture polish,
laundry detergent
Availability: health food
stores, distributors, mail order
V MO

Earth Science
475 N. Sheridan St.
Corona, CA 91720
909-371-7565
800-222-6720
Products: aromatherapy,
baby care, cosmetics,
fragrance, hair care,
dandruff shampoo, hair
color, hypo-allergenic skin
care for men and women,
sun care, bathing supply,
deodorant, shaving supply,
soap, vitamins
Availability: health food
stores, cooperatives, mail
order
★ ⬛ MO

Earth Solutions
1123 Zonolite Rd., #8
Atlanta, GA 30306
404-525-6167
800-883-3376
Products: baby care,
companion animal care,
natural hypo-allergenic
therapeutic skin care for
men, women, and children,
toiletries
Availability: health food
stores, cooperatives,
boutiques, specialty stores,
independent sales
representatives, mail order
V MO

Eberhard Faber (Sanford)
2711 Washington Blvd.
Bellwood, IL 60104
708-547-5525
800-438-3703
www.sanfordcorp.com
Products: office supply, ink,
writing instruments
Availability: department
stores, drugstores,
supermarkets, office supply
stores, mail order
MO

E. Burnham Cosmetics
7117 N. Austin Ave.
Niles, IL 60714
847-647-2121
Products: cosmetics, hair
care, hypo-allergenic skin
care for men and women
Availability: drugstores,
health food stores, mail order
MO

Ecco Bella Botanicals
1123 Route 23
Wayne, NJ 07470
973-696-7766
Products: aromatherapy,
cosmetics, fragrance, hair
care, dandruff shampoo,
household supply, air
freshener, hypo-allergenic
skin care, bathing supply,
shaving supply, soap
Availability: drugstores,
health food stores,
boutiques, specialty stores,
mail order
MO

Legend
V   Vegan (products
    contain no animal
    ingredients)
★   Company meets
    CSCA
⬛   Company uses
    Caring Consumer
    product logo
MO   Mail order
    available

Eco-DenT International
P.O. Box 5285
Redwood City, CA 94063-
0285
650-364-6343
888-ECO-DENT
Products: dental hygiene,
toothbrushes
Availability: drugstores,
health food stores,
supermarkets, cooperatives,
dentists, mail order
★ MO

Eco Design Company
1365 Rufina Cir.
Santa Fe, NM 87501
505-438-3448
800-621-2591
Products: companion animal
care, dental hygiene,
toothbrushes, furniture
polish, laundry detergent,
paint, wood finishing supply,
hypo-allergenic skin care,
bathing supply, shaving
supply, soap
Availability: environmentally
friendly stores, mail order
MO

Ecover
1166 Broadway, Suite L
Placerville, CA 95667
530-295-8400
800-449-4925
www.ecover.com
Products: household supply,
nonchlorine bleach, laundry
detergent, laundry detergent
for fine washables, dish
detergent, all-purpose
cleaner
Availability: health food
stores, supermarkets,
cooperatives, mail order
MO

Edward & Sons Trading Company
P.O. Box 1326
Carpinteria, CA 93014
805-684-8500
Products: household supply, hair care
Availability: health food stores, cooperatives, boutiques, specialty stores, mail order
MO

Elizabeth Grady Face First
200 Boston Ave., Suite 3500
Medford, MA 02155
617-391-9380
800-FACIALS
Products: cosmetics, nail care, hypo-allergenic skin care for men and women, sun care, toiletries
Availability: Elizabeth Grady Face First stores, boutiques, specialty stores, distributors, mail order
MO

Elizabeth Van Buren Aromatherapy
P.O. Box 7542
303 Potrero St., #33
Santa Cruz, CA 95061
408-425-8218
800-710-7759
Products: aromatherapy, hypo-allergenic skin care for women, essential oil, therapeutic blends, massage oil
Availability: department stores, drugstores, health food stores, metaphysical bookstores, massage therapists, mail order
V ★ MO

English Ideas, Ltd.
15251 Alton Pkwy.
Irvine, CA 92618
714-789-8790
800-547-5278
www.liplast.com
Products: personal care, Advanced Lip Technologies, nonprescription therapy
Availability: department stores, beauty supply stores, salons
★

Espial Corporation
7045 S. Fulton St., #200
Englewood, CO 80112-3700
303-799-0707
www.nomoreboss.com/products
Products: hair care, house-hold supply, skin care for men and women, toiletries
Availability: distributors, mail order
V ★ MO

Essential Aromatics
205 N. Signal St.
Ojai, CA 93023
805-640-1300
800-211-1313
www.essentialaromatics.com
Products: aromatherapy,
baby care, companion
animal care, fragrance, hair
care, skin care, essential oil
Availability: select stores,
mail order
V MO

The Essential Oil Company
1719 S.E. Umatilla St.
Portland, OR 97202
503-872-8772
800-729-5912
Products: aromatherapy, baby
care, fragrance for men and
women, insect repellant,
bathing supply, soap, essential
oil, soap-making supply
Availability: health food
stores, cooperatives,
herbalists, mail order
MO

**Essential Products of
America**
8702 N. Mobley Rd.
Odessa, FL 33556
813-920-2011
800-822-9698
Products: aromatherapy,
fragrance, air freshener,
hypo-allergenic skin care,
toiletries, bathing supply, soap,
essential oil, vegetable oil
Availability: health food
stores, boutiques, specialty
stores, salons, spas, health
care centers, mail order
V ★ MO

Estée Lauder
767 Fifth Ave.
New York, NY 10153
212-572-4200
Products: cosmetics, fragrance,
nail care, skin care, sun care,
toiletries, bathing supply,
deodorant, shaving supply,
soap, Clinique, Origins
Availability: department
stores, specialty stores

Eucerin (Beiersdorf)
BDF Plaza
360 Martin Luther King Dr.
Norwalk, CT 06856-5529
203-853-8008
Products: skin care
Availability: drugstores,
supermarket

European Gold
33 S.E. 11th St.
Grand Rapids, MN 55744
218-326-0266
800-946-5395
Products: hypo-allergenic
skin care for men and
women, sun care
Availability: tanning salons,
beauty salons, health clubs
(where tanning beds are used)

EuroZen
10 S. Franklin Tpk., #201
Ramsey, NJ 07446
201-447-0961
Products: aromatherapy, skin care, scented massage oil
Availability: independent sales representatives, mail order
V MO

Eva Jon Cosmetics
1016 E. California
Gainesville, TX 76240
817-668-7707
Products: cosmetics, toiletries
Availability: health food stores, spas, specialty shops, mail order
MO

Evans International
14 E. 15th St.
Richmond, VA 23224-0189
804-232-8946
800-368-3061
www.tackyfinger.com
Products: household supply, office supply, skin care, fingertip moistener, janitorial cleaning supply
Availability: office supply stores, office supply catalogs, mail order
MO

Every Body Ltd.
1738 Pearl St.
Boulder, CO 80302
303-440-0188
800-748-5675
Products: aromatherapy, baby care, cosmetics, dental hygiene, hair care, dandruff shampoo, hair color, air freshener, nail care, sun care, toiletries, bathing supply, deodorant, shaving supply, soap, massage oil
Availability: health food stores, supermarkets, cooperatives, Every Body Ltd. stores, boutiques, sports industry stores, mail order
MO

The Face Food Shoppe
21298 Pleasant Hill Rd.
Boonville, MO 65233
816-882-6858
800-882-6858
Products: aromatherapy, hypo-allergenic skin care for men and women, toiletries, bathing supply, shaving supply, soap, acne care
Availability: health food stores, cooperatives, The Face Food Shoppe store, independent sales representatives, mail order
MO

Faces by Gustavo
1200 N. Veitch St., Suite 812
Arlington, VA 22201
703-908-9620
800-58-FACE1
Products: aromatherapy, baby care, cosmetics, hypo-allergenic skin care, sun care, toiletries, soap
Availability: Faces by Gustavo stores, boutiques, specialty stores, salons, mail order
MO

Facets/Crystalline Cosmetics
8436 N. 80th Place
Scottsdale, AZ 85258
602-991-1704
Products: skin care for men and women
Availability: mail order
MO

Faith Products, Ltd.
Unit 5, Kay St.
Bury Lancashire BL9 6BU
England
161-7642555
www.faithproducts.com
Products: aromatherapy, baby care, hair care, laundry detergent for fine washables, skin care for men and women, toiletries, bathing supply, soap
Availability: health food stores, mail order
MO

Farmavita USA (Chuckles)
P.O. Box 5126
Manchester, NH 03109
603-669-4228
800-221-3496
Products: hair color
Availability: salons

Faultless Starch/Bon Ami
510 Walnut St.
Kansas City, MO 64106-1209
816-842-1230
Products: household supply
Availability: drugstores, supermarkets

Fernand Aubry
14, rue Alexandre Parodi
75010 Paris
France
1-42-05-83-79
Products: cosmetics, fragrance for men and women, nail care, skin care for men and women, toiletries
Availability: department stores, boutiques, specialty stores, salons, spas

Fleabusters/Rx For Fleas
6555 N.W. Ninth Ave.
Suite 412
Ft. Lauderdale, FL 33309
954-351-9244
800-666-3532
www.fleabuster.com
Products: insect repellant
Availability: cooperatives, independent sales representatives, mail order
★ MO

Flower Essences of Fox Mountain
P.O. Box 381
Worthington, MA 01098
413-238-4291
Products: vibrational medicine, holistic health care, nonprescription therapy
Availability: health food stores, supermarkets, bookstores, mail order
V MO

Focus 21 International
2755 Dos Aarons Way
Vista, CA 92083
619-727-6626
800-832-2887
Products: hair care
Availability: salons

Food Lion
P.O. Box 1330
Salisbury, NC 28145-1330
704-633-8250
www.foodlion.com
Products: baby care, hair care, household supply, nail care, office supplies, razors, skin care, toiletries, vitamins
Availability: Food Lion stores

Forest Essentials
601 Del Norte Blvd., Suite F
Channel Islands, CA 93030
805-278-8975
800-301-7767
www.forestessentials.com
Products: fragrance for women, hair and skin care for men and women, sun care, toiletries, body and skin care gifts
Availability: department stores, beauty supply stores, environmentally friendly stores, gift shops, mail order
MO

Forever Living Products International
7501 E. McCormick Pkwy.
Scottsdale, AZ 85258
602-998-8888
Products: aromatherapy, companion animal care, cosmetics, dental hygiene, hair care, household supply, laundry detergent, skin care, bathing supply, deodorant, shaving supply, soap, nutritional drinks
Availability: independent sales representatives, mail order
MO

Forever New International
4701 N. Fourth Ave.
Sioux Falls, SD 57104-0403
605-331-2910
800-456-0107
www.forevernew.com
Products: advanced care formulations for fine washables
Availability: department stores, boutiques, specialty stores, mail order
V ★ MO

For Pet's Sake Enterprises
3780 Eastway Rd., Suite 10A
South Euclid, OH 44118
216-932-8810
800-285-0298
Products: aromatherapy, baby care, cosmetics, fragrance, hair care, dandruff shampoo, household supply, car care, nail care, skin care, toiletries, deodorant, vitamins
Availability: distributors, mail order
▨ MO

Fragrance Impressions, Ltd.
116 Knowlton St.
Bridgeport, CT 06608
203-367-6995
800-541-3204
Products: fragrance for men and women
Availability: drugstores, supermarkets

Framesi USA
400 Chess St.
Coraopolis, PA 15108
412-269-2950
800-321-9648
Products: hair care, hair color, permanents
Availability: salons

Frank T. Ross (Nature Clean)
6550 Lawrence Ave. E.
Scarborough, ON M1C 4A7
Canada
416-282-1107
Products: hair care, household supply, bleach, car care, carpet cleaning supply, laundry detergent, glue, soap
Availability: department stores, drugstores, health food stores, supermarkets, cooperatives, mail order
V MO

Freeda Vitamins
36 E. 41st St.
New York, NY 10017
212-685-4980
800-777-3737
Products: vitamins and nutrients
Availability: drugstores, health food stores, cooperatives, Freeda Vitamin stores, mail order
MO

Free Spirit Enterprises
P.O. Box 2638
Guerneville, CA 95446
707-869-1942
Products: skin care for men
and women, massage lotion
Availability: health food
stores, cooperatives, boutiques,
specialty stores, mail order
V MO

French Transit
398 Beach Rd.
Burlingame, CA 94010
650-548-9000
800-829-7625
www.thecrystal.com
Products: hypo-allergenic
skin care, toiletries, bathing
supply, deodorant
Availability: department
stores, drugstores, health
food stores, boutiques,
specialty stores, mail order
V ☆ MO

**Frontier Natural Products
Co-op**
3021 78th St.
Box 299
Norway, IA 52318
319-227-7996
800-669-3275
Products: aromatherapy,
fragrance, household supply,
toiletries, bathing supply,
soap, vitamins, herbs
Availability: health food
stores, cooperatives, mail
order
V MO

Fruit of the Earth
P.O. Box 152044
Irving, TX 75015-2044
972-790-0808
800-527-7731
Products: hair care, skin
care, sun care
Availability: discount
department stores,
drugstores, supermarkets

Garden Botanika
8624 154th Ave. N.E.
Redmond, WA 98052
425-881-9603
800-968-7842
www.gardenbotanika.com
Products: cosmetics,
fragrance, hair care, nail
care, skin care for men and
women, sun care, toiletries,
bathing supply, deodorant,
shaving supply, soap,
vitamins, herbs
Availability: Garden
Botanika stores, mail order,
Web site
MO

Garnier
575 Fifth Ave.
New York, NY 10017
212-818-1500
Products: hair color
Availability: supermarkets,
drugstores

Georgette Klinger
501 Madison Ave.
New York, NY 10022
212-838-3200
800-KLINGER
Products: cosmetics,
fragrance for men and
women, hair care, nail care,
skin care, sun care, toiletries,
bathing supply, shaving
supply, soap
Availability: Georgette
Klinger salons, specialty
stores, mail order
MO

Gigi Laboratories
2220 Gaspar Ave.
Los Angeles, CA 90040
213-728-2999
Products: skin care for
women
Availability: boutiques,
specialty stores, beauty
supply stores

Giovanni Cosmetics
5415 Tweedy Blvd.
Southgate, CA 90280
213-563-0355
800-563-5468
Products: hair care
Availability: drugstores, health
food stores, supermarkets,
cooperatives, boutiques,
specialty stores, mail order
V MO

Golden Pride/Rawleigh
1501 Northpoint Pkwy.
Suite 100
West Palm Beach, FL 33407
407-640-5700
Products: cosmetics, hair
care, household supply,
furniture polish, laundry
detergent, skin care, sun
care, shaving supply, soap,
vitamins
Availability: independent
sales representatives, mail
order
MO

Goldwell Cosmetics (USA)
981 Corporate Blvd.
Linthicum, MD 21090
301-725-6620
800-288-9118
Products: hair care, hair
color
Availability: salons

Green Ban
P.O. Box 146
Norway, IA 52318
319-446-7495
Products: companion animal
care, insect repellant,
insect-bite treatment
Availability: health food
stores, cooperatives,
specialty stores, sporting
goods stores, mail order
V MO

Greentree Laboratories
P.O. Box 425
Tustin, CA 92681
714-546-9520
Products: companion
animal care
Availability: companion
animal supply stores, mail
order
MO

Gryphon Development
666 Fifth Ave.
New York, NY 10103
212-582-1220
Products: fragrance,
personal care, toiletries,
Victoria's Secret, Bath &
Body Works, Abercrombie &
Fitch, Henri Bendel
Availability: Victoria's
Secret, Bath & Body Works,
Abercrombie & Fitch,
Henri Bendel

Halo, Purely for Pets
3438 E. Lake Rd., #14
Palm Harbor, FL 34685
813-854-2214
www.halopets.com
Products: companion animal
care, insect repellant
Availability: companion
animal supply stores, health
food stores, mail order
MO

Hard Candy
110 N. Doheny Dr.
Beverly Hills, CA 90211
310-275-8099
Products: cosmetics, nail care
Availability: department
stores, boutiques

Hargen Distributing
4015 N. 40th Place
Phoenix, AZ 85018
602-381-0799
Products: deodorant stones
Availability: health food
stores, mail order
V MO

Hawaiian Resources Co., Ltd.
68-309 Crozier Dr.
Waialua, HI 96791
808-636-2300
www.pete.com/monoioil
Products: hypo-allergenic
skin care for men and women,
sun care, toiletries, soap
Availability: department
stores, drugstores, health
food stores, boutiques,
specialty stores, Web site
V ✴

The Health Catalog
1727 Cosmic Way
Glendale, CA 91201
818-790-1776
800-523-8899
www.healthcatalog.com
Products: vitamins, herbs
Availability: health food
stores, mail order
MO

**HealthRite/Montana
Naturals**
19994 Highway 93 N.
Arlee, MT 59821
406-726-3214
www.mtnaturals.com
Products: herbs, specialty
supplements
Availability: drugstores,
health food stores, supermarkets, cooperatives, Montana
Naturals stores, boutiques,
specialty stores, mail order,
Web site
✴ MO

Healthy Times
13200 Kirkham Way
Suite 104
Poway, CA 92064
619-513-1550
Products: baby care
Availability: health food
stores, cooperatives, baby
stores, mail order
V MO

**Helen Lee Skin Care and
Cosmetics**
205 E. 60th St.
New York, NY 10022
212-888-1233
800-288-1077
www.helenlee.com
Products: cosmetics,
fragrance for women, hair
care, nail care, hypo-allergenic
skin care for men and women,
sun care, toiletries, bathing
supply, shaving supply, soap,
vitamins, herbs
Availability: Helen Lee Day
Spas, mail order
MO

Henri Bendel
712 Fifth Ave.
New York, NY 10019
212-247-1100
Products: fragrance for women
Availability: Henri Bendel
stores, mail order
MO

**Herbal Products &
Development**
P.O. Box 1084
Aptos, CA 95001
831-688-8706
Products: vitamins, herbs,
herbal supplements
Availability: health food
stores, mail order
✴ MO

The Herb Garden
P.O. Box 773-P
Pilot Mountain, NC 27041
910-368-2723
Products: aromatherapy,
companion animal care,
fragrance, insect repellant,
skin care, soap, vitamins,
herbs
Availability: farmers'
markets, mail order
V MO

H.e.r.c. Consumer Products
2538 N. Sandy Creek Dr.
Westlake Village, CA 91361
818-991-9985
Products: household supply
Availability: health food
stores, home centers and
hardware stores, mail order
V MO

The Hewitt Soap Company
333 Linden Ave.
Dayton, OH 45403
513-253-1151
800-543-2245
Products: companion animal
care, fragrance for men and
women, toiletries
Availability: department
stores, discount department
stores, drugstores, health
food stores, boutiques,
specialty stores, distributors,
mail order
MO

Hobé Laboratories
4032 E. Broadway
Phoenix, AZ 85040
602-257-1950
800-528-4482
Products: hair care, skin care
for men and women, hair
loss and scalp problem
shampoo, psoriasis
treatment, supplements,
weight loss tea, topical
analgesic, instant hand/hard
surface sanitizers
Availability: department
stores, drugstores, health
food stores, supermarkets,
cooperatives, boutiques,
specialty stores, mail order
MO

Homebody (Perfumoils)
143A Main St.
Brattleboro, VT 05301
802-254-6280
Products: fragrance for men
and women, hair care,
hypo-allergenic skin care for
men and women, toiletries,
shaving supply, soap
Availability: Homebody stores
🖾

Home Health Products
P.O. Box 8425
Virginia Beach, VA 23450
757-468-3130
800-284-9123
Products: aromatherapy,
companion animal care,
dental hygiene, feminine
hygiene, hair care, dandruff
shampoo, hair color,
household supply, insect
repellant, nail care, skin care,
toiletries, vitamins, herbs
Availability: health food
stores, cooperatives, mail
order
MO

**Home Service Products
Company**
P.O. Box 129
Lambertville, NJ 08530
609-397-8674
Products: laundry detergent,
laundry detergent for fine
washables
Availability: mail order
V ★ MO

House of Cheriss
13475 Holiday Dr.
Saratoga, CA 95070
408-867-6795
Products: ayurvedic skin
care for men and women,
cleansing cream, washing
grains, toner, moisturizer,
body lotion, hair oil, travel
packs, massage cream, masks
Availability: health food and
specialty stores in San
Francisco Bay area, mail
order
MO

H2O Plus
845 W. Madison
Chicago, IL 60607
312-850-9283
800-242-BATH
Products: baby and child
care, cosmetics,
toothbrushes, fragrance for
men and women, hair care,
nail care, skin care for men
and women, sun care,
toiletries, shaving supply,
toys
Availability: department
stores, H2O Plus stores,
boutiques, specialty stores,
duty-free shops, mail order
MO

Huish Detergents
3540 W. 1987 S.
P.O. Box 25057
Salt Lake City, UT 84125
801-975-3100
800-776-6702
www.huish.com
Products: household supply,
floor finish, disinfectant,
window cleaner, dish
detergent
Availability: department
stores, discount department
stores, drugstores,
supermarkets

Ida Grae (Nature's Colors Cosmetics)
424 La Verne Ave.
Mill Valley, CA 94941
415-388-6101
Products: cosmetics,
hypo-allergenic skin care for
men and women, *Nature's
Colors: Dyes From Plants*
Availability: health food
stores, cooperatives,
i natural stores, boutiques,
specialty stores, mail order

Il-Makiage
107 E. 60th St.
New York, NY 10022
800-722-1011
Products: cosmetics, hair
care, hair color, nail care,
hypo-allergenic skin care
for women
Availability: cooperatives,
Il-Makiage stores, boutiques,
specialty stores, salons,
health spas, mail order

ILONA
3201 E. Second Ave.
Denver, CO 80206-5203
303-322-3000
888-38-ILONA
www.ilona.com
Products: cosmetics,
fragrance for men and
women, skin care for men
and women, sun care
Availability: department
stores, Ilona stores, boutiques,
specialty stores, mail order,
Web site

i natural cosmetics (Cosmetic Source)
32-02 Queen's Blvd.
Long Island City, NY 11101
718-729-2929
800-962-5387
Products: cosmetics, hair
care, hypo-allergenic skin
care for men and women,
sun care, toiletries, shaving
supply
Availability: i natural stores,
General Nutrition Centers

Innovative Formulations
1810 S. Sixth Ave.
S. Tucson, AZ 85713
520-628-1553
Products: paint, coatings for
roof, household supply,
roofing material,
architectural paint, nail
polish remover
Availability: mail order

International Rotex
7171 Telegraph Rd.
Los Angeles, CA 90040-
3227
Products: office supply,
correction fluid
Availability: discount
department stores,
drugstores, supermarkets,
cooperatives, wholesale
distributors

International Vitamin Corporation
209 40th St.
Irvington, NJ 07111
201-371-7300
Products: vitamins
Availability: health food
stores, mail order

InterNatural
P.O. Box 1008
Silver Lake, WI 53170
414-889-8501
800-548-3824
www.internatural.com
Products: aromatherapy,
condoms, cosmetics, dental
care, feminine hygiene,
dandruff shampoo, hair
color, furniture polish,
laundry detergent, insect
repellant, nail care, skin
care, sun care, toiletries,
herbs
Availability: mail order,
Web site

IQ Products Company
16212 State Hwy. 249
Houston, TX 77086
281-444-6454
Products: hair care, insect
repellent, car care, cleaning
supply
Availability: discount
department stores,
drugstores, supermarkets

Island Dog Cosmetics
3 Milltown Ct.
Union, NJ 07083
908-851-0330
Products: cosmetics

IV Trail Products
P.O. Box 1033
Sykesville, MD 21784
410-795-8989
Products: companion animal
care for horses
Availability: mail order
V MO

Jacki's Magic Lotion
258 A St., #7A
Ashland, OR 97520
541-488-1388
Products: aromatherapy,
baby care, ethnic personal
care, skin care for men and
women, toiletries, shaving
supply, massage lotion
Availability: health food
stores, cooperatives, mail order
MO

James Austin Company
P.O. Box 827
115 Downieville Rd.
Mars, PA 16046
724-625-1535
800-245-1942
Products: laundry detergent,
oven cleaner, bleach, carpet
cleaning supply, glass
cleaner, multipurpose
cleaner, household supply
Availability: discount
department stores,
drugstores, supermarkets

Jane (Estée Lauder)
767 Fifth Ave.
New York, NY 10153
212-572-4200
Products: cosmetics
Availability: department
stores, drugstores

Jason Natural Cosmetics
8468 Warner Dr.
Culver City, CA 90232-2484
310-838-7543
800-JASON-05
www.jason-natural.com
Products: aromatherapy,
feminine hygiene, fragrance,
hair care, dandruff shampoo,
hair color, insect repellant,
hypo-allergenic skin care,
sun care, bathing supply,
deodorant, shaving supply,
soap
Availability: health food
stores, cooperatives, mail
order, Web site
★ MO

J.C. Garet
2471 Coral St.
Vista, CA 92083
619-598-0505
800-548-9770
Products: household supply,
laundry soap
Availability: department
stores, drugstores, health
food stores, supermarkets,
cooperatives, boutiques,
uniform stores, distributors,
mail order
MO

Jeanne Rose Aromatherapy
219 Carl St.
San Francisco, CA 94117-
3804
415-564-6785
Products: aromatherapy,
companion animal care,
hypo-allergenic skin care for
men and women, toiletries,
herbs, oil
Availability: health food
stores, cooperatives,
boutiques, specialty stores,
independent sales representatives, mail order
MO

Jennifer Tara Cosmetics
775 E. Blithedale, #195
Mill Valley, CA 94941
800-818-8272
Products: cosmetics, skin care
Availability: mail order
★ MO

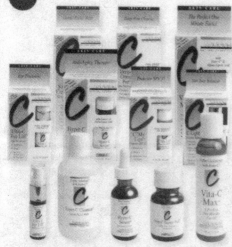

Jessica McClintock
1400 16th St.
San Francisco, CA 94103-5181
415-553-8200
800-333-5301
Products: fragrance for
women
Availability: department
stores, Jessica McClintock
boutiques, mail order
MO

Jheri Redding (Conair)
1 Cummings Point Rd.
Stamford, CT 06904
203-351-9000
800-7-CONAIR
Products: hair care,
permanents, toiletries,
Conair hair-care styling tools
Availability: discount
department stores,
drugstores, supermarkets,
beauty supply stores,

Joe Blasco Cosmetics
7340 Greenbriar Pkwy.
Orlando, FL 32819
407-363-7070
800-553-1520
www.joeblasco.com
Products: cosmetics
Availability: Joe Blasco
stores, boutiques, specialty
stores, beauty supply stores,
salons, spas, mail order
MO

**John Amico Expressive Hair
Care Products**
4731 W. 136th St.
Crestwood, IL 60445
708-824-4000
800-676-5264
www.johnamico.com
Products: ethnic personal
care, hair care, dandruff
shampoo, hair color,
permanents, vitamins, herbs
Availability: salons, mail order
 MO

John Paul Mitchell Systems
9701 Wilshire Blvd.
Suite 1205
Beverly Hills, CA 90212
310-248-3888
800-321-JPMS
Products: hair care, skin
care, sun care
Availability: salons
 V ★

JOICO Laboratories
P.O. Box 42308
Los Angeles, CA 90042-0308
626-968-6111
800-44-JOICO
www.joico.com
Products: hair care, hair
color, permanents
Availability: salons
V

Jolen Creme Bleach
25 Walls Dr.
P.O. Box 458
Fairfield, CT 06430
203-259-8779
Products: Jolen Creme
Bleach for facial and body
hair
Availability: discount
department stores,
supermarkets, drugstores

J.R. Liggett, Ltd.
R.R. 2, Box 911
Cornish, NH 03745
603-675-2055
www.jrliggett.com
Products: hair care, dandruff
shampoo
Availability: drugstores, health
food stores, cooperatives,
boutiques, specialty stores,
independent sales
representatives, mail order
V ★ **MO**

Jurlique Cosmetics
1000 Holcombe Woods
Pkwy., Suite 318
Roswell, GA 30076
770-643-6999
800-854-1110
Products: baby care,
cosmetics, hair care,
dandruff oil, household
supply, sun care, toiletries
Availability: salons, spas,
mail order
MO

Katonah Scentral
51 Katonah Ave.
Katonah, NY 10536
914-232-7519
800-29-SCENT
Products: aromatherapy,
baby care, dental hygiene,
toothbrushes, fragrance for
men and women, hair care,
hair color, toiletries, shaving
supply, essential oil
Availability: Katonah
Scentral stores, mail order
 MO

K.B. Products
20 N. Railroad Ave.
San Mateo, CA 94401
415-344-6500
800-342-4321
Products: companion animal
care, hair care, dandruff
shampoo, hand lotion
Availability: companion
animal supply stores, K.B.
stores, mail order
MO

Kenic Pet Products
109 S. Main St.
Lawrenceburg, KY 40342
800-228-7387
Products: companion
animal care
Availability: drugstores,
health food stores,
independent sales representatives, companion animal
supply stores, grooming
stores, hardware stores,
veterinarians, mail order
MO

**Ken Lange No-Thio
Permanent Waves & Hair**
7112 N. 15th Place, Suite 1
Phoenix, AZ 85020
800-486-3033
Products: hair care,
permanents
Availability: salons
V

Kenra
6501 Julian Ave.
Indianapolis, IN 46219
317-356-6491
800-428-8073
Products: ethnic personal
care, hair care
Availability: salons

Kiehl's Since 1851
109 Third Ave.
New York, NY 10003
973-244-9828
800-KIEHLS1
Products: baby care,
cosmetics, fragrance for men
and women, hair care, skin
care, sun care
Availability: department
stores, Kiehl's stores, mail
order
MO

Kiss My Face
P.O. Box 224
144 Main St.
Gardiner, NY 12525
914-255-0884
800-262-KISS
www.kissmyface.com
Products: baby care,
cosmetics, hair care, skin
care for men and women,
sun care, toiletries, shaving
supply
Availability: drugstores, health
food stores, cooperatives,
boutiques, massage
therapists, salons, mail order
★ MO

Kleen Brite Laboratories
200 State St.
Brockport, NY 14420
716-637-0630
800-223-1473
Products: household supply,
bleach, laundry detergent for
fine washables
Availability: drugstores,
supermarkets, cooperatives

KMS Research
4712 Mountain Lakes Blvd.
Redding, CA 96003
916-244-6000
800-DIAL-KMS
www.kmshaircare.com
Products: hair care, dandruff
shampoo, permanents
Availability: salons

KSA Jojoba
19025 Parthenia St., #200
Northridge, CA 91324
818-701-1534
www.jojoba-ksa.com
Products: aromatherapy,
baby care, companion
animal care, cosmetics,
fragrance, hair care, skin
care, sun care, toiletries,
bathing supply, soap
Availability: mail order
V ★ MO

**La Costa Products
International**
2875 Loker Ave. E.
Carlsbad, CA 92008
619-438-2181
800-LA-COSTA
Products: cosmetics, hair
care, nail care, skin care for
women, sun care, toiletries,
shaving supply
Availability: salons, mail order
MO

La Crista
P.O. Box 240
Davidsonville, MD 21035
410-956-4447
800-888-2231
www.Lacrista.com
Products: aromatherapy,
baby care, hypo-allergenic
skin care for men and
women, toiletries, soap
Availability: drugstores,
health food stores,
supermarkets, specialty
stores, mail order, Web site
V ▤ MO

Lady of the Lake
P.O. Box 7140
Brookings, OR 97415
541-469-3354
Products: aromatherapy,
homeopathic remedies, water
treatment systems, books
Availability: health food
stores, independent sales
representatives, mail order
V ⭐ MO

LaNatura
425 N. Bedford Dr.
Beverly Hills, CA 90210
310-271-5616
800-352-6288
Products: baby care,
cosmetics, fragrance for
women, skin care, toiletries,
bathing supply, soap
Availability: health food
stores, LaNatura stores,
boutiques, specialty stores,
hotel private label, mail order
V MO

Lancôme
575 Fifth Ave.
New York, NY 10017
212-818-1500
Products: cosmetics, sun care
Availability: department
stores

Lander Co.
106 Grand Ave.
Englewood, NJ 07631
201-568-9700
800-4-LANDER
www.lander-hbc.com
Products: baby care, ethnic
personal care, hair care,
dandruff shampoo, toiletries,
bathing supply, shaving
supply
Availability: discount
department stores,
drugstores, supermarkets

**L'anza Research
International**
935 W. Eighth St.
Azusa, CA 91702
818-334-9333
800-423-0307
Products: hair care, dandruff
shampoo, hair color,
permanents
Availability: salons
V

La Prairie
31 W. 52nd St.
New York, NY 10019
212-459-1600
800-821-5718
Products: cosmetics,
fragrance for men and
women, skin care for
women, sun care
Availability: department
stores, boutiques, specialty
stores

From nature
without cruelty.

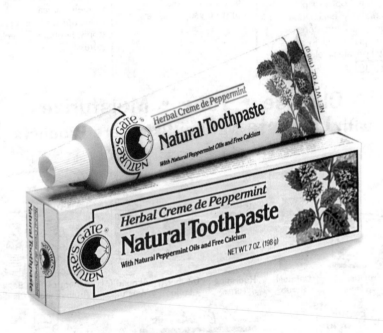

Lee Pharmaceuticals
1434 Santa Anita Ave.
S. El Monte, CA 91733
818-442-3141
800-950-5337
Products: nail care, Lee
acrylic nails, Nose Better,
Zip hair removal, Saxon
aftershave cream, Sundance
aloe, Peterson's ointment,
Creamalin antacid, Bikini
Bare depilatory
Availability: drugstores,
supermarkets, boutiques

**Levlad/Nature's Gate
Herbal Cosmetics**
9200 Mason Ave.
Chatsworth, CA 91311
818-882-2951
800-327-2012
www.levlad.com
Products: aromatherapy,
dental hygiene, hair care,
hypo-allergenic skin care for
women, sun care, bathing
supply, deodorant, shaving
supply, soap
Availability: discount
department stores, health
food stores, supermarkets,
mail order
★ MO

Liberty Natural Products
8120 S.E. Stock St.
Portland, OR 97215-2346
503-256-1227
800-289-8427
www.libertynatural.com
Products: aromatherapy,
baby care, dental hygiene,
fragrance, hair care,
household supply, air
freshener, insect repellant,
nail care, skin care,
toiletries, bathing supply,
deodorant, soap, vitamins
Availability: discount
department stores,
drugstores, health food
stores, supermarkets,
cooperatives, boutiques,
specialty stores
V

Life Dynamics
8512 Baxter Place
Burnaby, BC V5A 4T8
Canada
800-977-9664
Products: hair care, hypo-
allergenic skin care for men
and women, toiletries,
natural color protection
Availability: specialty stores,
distributors, mail order
MO

Life Tree Products
P.O. Box 1203
Sebastopol, CA 95473
707-588-0755
Products: laundry detergent,
toiletries, bathing supply,
soap, all-purpose cleaning
supply, dish detergent
Availability: drugstores,
health food stores,
supermarkets, cooperatives,
mail order
V MO

Lightning Products
1900 Erie St.
N. Kansas City, MO 64116
816-221-3183
Products: companion animal
care, household supply,
carpet cleaning supply
Availability: health food
stores, companion animal
supply stores, mail order
MO

Lily of Colorado
P.O. Box 12471
Denver, CO 80212
303-455-4194
Products: purely botanical
skin care
Availability: health food
stores, mail order
MO

**Lime-O-Sol Company
(The Works)**
P.O. Box 395
Ashley, IN 46705
219-587-9151
Products: household supply,
drain opener
Availability: department
stores, discount department
stores, drugstores,
supermarkets

**Little Forest Natural Baby
Products**
2415 Third St., Suite #238
San Francisco, CA 94107
415-621-6504
888-329-BABY
www.littleforest.com
Products: baby care
Availability: health food
stores, baby boutiques,
independent sales
representatives, mail order
V ★ MO

Liz Claiborne Cosmetics
1441 Broadway
New York, NY 10018
212-354-4900
Products: fragrance, toiletries, bathing supply, deodorant, shaving supply, soap
Availability: department stores, Liz Claiborne stores

Lobob Laboratories
1440 Atteberry La.
San Jose, CA 95131-1410
408-432-0580
800-83LOBOB
www.loboblabs.com
Products: hard and soft contact lens cleaner, wetting solution, soaking solution
Availability: discount department stores, drugstores, supermarkets, mail order
V ★ ⬛ MO

Logona USA
554-E Riverside Dr.
Asheville, NC 28801
704-252-1420
Products: baby care, dental hygiene, fragrance for men, hair care, dandruff shampoo, hair color, hypo-allergenic skin care for men and women, sun care, toiletries, shaving supply
Availability: health food stores, cooperatives, boutiques, specialty stores, mail order
MO

L'Oréal (Cosmair)
575 Fifth Ave.
New York, NY 10017
212-818-1500
www.lorealcosmetics.com
Products: cosmetics, hair care, fragrance for men and women, hair color, permanents, nail care, hypo-allergenic skin care for men and women, toiletries
Availability: department stores, discount department stores, drugstores, supermarkets, boutiques, specialty stores

Legend
V   Vegan (products contain no animal ingredients)
★   Company meets CSCA
⬛   Company uses Caring Consumer product logo
MO   Mail order available

Lotus Light
1100 Lotus Dr.
Silver Lake, WI 53170
414-889-8501
800-548-3824
Products: aromatherapy,
baby care, companion
animal care, condoms,
lubricants, cosmetics, dental
hygiene, toothbrushes,
feminine hygiene, fragrance,
hair care, insect repellant,
skin care, soap, vitamins,
herbs
Availability: drugstores,
health food stores,
supermarkets, cooperatives,
specialty stores, mail order
MO

Louise Bianco Skin Care
13655 Chandler Blvd.
Sherman Oaks, CA 91401
818-786-2700
800-782-3067
www.louisebianco.com
Products: hypo-allergenic
skin care for men and
women, sun care, toiletries,
bathing supply, deodorant
Availability: salons, mail
order, Web site
MO

M.A.C. Cosmetics
233 Carlton St., Suite 201
Toronto, ON M5A 2L2
Canada
416-924-0598
800-387-6707
Products: cosmetics, ethnic
personal care, hair care, nail
care, hypo-allergenic skin
care for men and women,
theatrical makeup
Availability: department
stores, M.A.C. Cosmetics
stores

Magick Botanicals
3412 W. MacArthur Blvd., #K
Santa Ana, CA 92704
714-957-0674
800-237-0674
Products: baby care, hair
care, skin care for men and
women, toiletries
Availability: health food
stores, mail order
MO

The Magic of Aloe
7300 N. Crescent Blvd.
Pennsauken, NJ 08110
856-662-3334
800-257-7770
www.magicofaloe.com
Products: cosmetics, hair
care, skin care for men and
women, sun care, toiletries,
bathing supply, shaving
supply, soap, vitamins
Availability: independent
sales representatives, salons,
mail order, Web site
MO

Mallory Pet Supplies
118 Atrisco Dr. S.W.
Albuquerque, NM 87105
505-836-4033
800-824-4464
Products: companion
animal care
Availability: companion
animal supply stores, mail
order
MO

**Manic Panic (Tish &
Snooky's)**
64-66 White St., 3rd Fl.
New York, NY 10013
212-941-0656
800-95-MANIC
Products: cosmetics, hair
bleach, hair color, nail care
Availability: department
stores, drugstores, health
food stores, mail order
MO

Marcal Paper Mills
1 Market St.
Elmwood Park, NJ 07407
201-796-4000
www.marcalpaper.com
Products: household paper,
toilet paper
Availability: drugstores,
supermarkets
V

Marché Image Corporation
P.O. Box 1010
Bronxville, NY 10708
914-793-2093
800-753-9980
Products: hypo-allergenic
skin care for men and
women, sun care
Availability: independent
sales representatives, mail
order
MO

Marilyn Miglin Institute
112 E. Oak St.
Chicago, IL 60611
312-943-1120
800-662-1120
Products: cosmetics, fragrance
for men and women, skin care
Availability: Marilyn Miglin
Institute, sales consultants,
mail order
MO

Mary Kay
16251 Dallas Pkwy.
Dallas, TX 75248-2696
972-687-6300
800-MARYKAY
www.marykay.com
Products: cosmetics,
fragrance, nail care, skin
care, sun care, bathing
supply, vitamins
Availability: independent
sales representatives

Masada Marketing Company
P.O. Box 4118
Chatsworth, CA 91313
818-717-8300
800-368-8811
www.masada-spa.com
Products: Dead Sea mineral bath salts
Availability: health food stores, cooperatives, mail order
V MO

Mastey de Paris
25413 Rye Canyon Rd.
Valencia, CA 91355
805-257-4814
800-6-MASTEY
Products: hair care, dandruff shampoo, hair color, permanents, skin care, sun care, toiletries
Availability: salons, beauty schools, mail order
MO

Maybelline
P.O. Box 1010
Clark, NJ 07066
800-944-0730
Products: cosmetics, ethnic personal care
Availability: drugstores, supermarkets

Mehron
100 Red Schoolhouse Rd.
Chestnut Ridge, NY 10977
914-426-1700
800-332-9955
Products: cosmetics, theatrical makeup
Availability: boutiques, specialty stores, party supply stores, costume stores, mail order
MO

Mère Cie
1100 Soscol Ferry Rd., Suite 3
Napa, CA 94558
707-257-8510
800-832-4544
www.merecie.com
Products: aromatherapy, fragrance for men and women
Availability: department stores, drugstores, health food stores, boutiques, specialty stores, independent sales representatives, mail order
MO

Merle Norman
9130 Bellanca Ave.
Los Angeles, CA 90045
310-641-3000
www.merlenorman.com
Products: cosmetics, skin care
Availability: Merle Norman salons

Mia Rose Products
177-F Riverside Ave.
Newport Beach, CA 92663
714-662-5465
800-292-6339
www.miarose.com
Products: aromatherapy, household supply
Availability: drugstores, health food stores, supermarkets, cooperatives, boutiques, specialty stores, distributors, mail order
V ☆ 🏠 MO

Michael's Naturopathic Programs
6203 Woodlake Ctr.
San Antonio, TX 78244
210-661-8311
800-525-9643
www.michaelshealth.com
Products: cosmetics, insect repellant, skin care, vitamins, herbs
Availability: health food stores
☆

Michelle Lazar Cosmetics
755 S. Lugo Ave.
San Bernardino, CA 92048
909-888-6310
Products: skin care
Availability: health food stores, mail order
MO

Micro Balanced Products
20 Foster St.
P.O. Box 8
Bergenfield, NJ 07621
201-387-0200
800-626-7888
Products: hypo-allergenic skin care for men and women, sun care, toiletries
Availability: health food stores, mail order
V MO

Mill Creek Botanicals
620 Airpark Rd.
Napa, CA 94558
800-447-6758
www.millcreekbotanicals.com
Products: hair care, dandruff shampoo, skin care for women, sun care, toiletries, bathing supply, deodorant, shaving supply, soap, vitamins, herbs
Availability: drugstores, health food stores, supermarkets

Mira Linder Spa in the City
29935 Northwestern Hwy.
Southfield, MI 48034
800-321-8860
Products: cosmetics, nail care, hypo-allergenic skin care for men and women
Availability: Mira Linder Spa in the City stores, mail order
MO

Montagne Jeunesse
Eco-Factory, Off Valley Way
Llansamlet, Swansea
SA6 8QP Wales,
Great Britain
01792-310306
Products: aromatherapy, skin
care for women, toiletries,
bathing supply, soap,
lotions, depilatory
Availability: department
stores, discount department
stores, drugstores, health
food stores, supermarkets,
cooperatives, boutiques,
specialty stores, independent
sales representatives
★

**Montana Naturals/
HealthRite**
19994 Hwy. 93 N.
Arlee, MT 59821
406-726-3214
800-872-7218
www.mtnaturals.com
Products: herbs, specialty
supplements
Availability: drugstores,
health food stores,
supermarkets, cooperatives,
Montana Naturals stores,
boutiques, specialty stores,
mail order, Web site
★ MO

Mother's Little Miracle
27520 Hawthorne Blvd.
Suite 125
Rolling Hills Estates, CA
90274
310-544-7125
Products: baby care,
children's stain and odor
remover and prewash, spit-
up remover, air freshener
Availability: drugstores,
discount department stores,
boutiques, specialty stores,
distributors, mail order
V MO

Mountain Ocean Ltd.
5150 Valmont Rd.
Boulder, CO 80306
303-444-2781
Products: baby care
(prenatal), hair care, toiletries
Availability: health food
stores, supermarkets, mail
order
MO

51

Mr. Christal's
10877 Wilshire Blvd., 12th Fl.
Los Angeles, CA 90024
310-824-2508
800-426-0108
www.mrchristals.com
Products: companion
animal care
Availability: mail order
MO

Murad
2121 Rosecrans Ave.
El Segundo, Ca 90245
310-726-3344
Products: hair care, dandruff
shampoo, hypo-allergenic
skin care, sun care
Availability: Murad stores,
mail order

Nadina's Cremes
3600 Clipper Mill Rd.
Suite 140
Baltimore, MD 21211
410-235-9192
800-722-4292
Products: scented body
cream for men and women,
body care
Availability: drugstores, health
food stores, cooperatives,
boutiques, specialty stores,
independent sales
representatives, environmentally friendly stores, New
Age stores, mail order
★ MO

Nala Barry Labs
P.O. Box 151
Palm Desert, CA 92261
619-321-7098
800-397-4174
Products: companion animal
care, nutritional supplements
Availability: health food
stores, cooperatives,
boutiques, specialty stores,
companion animal supply
stores, garden shops
V 🖾

Narwhale of High Tor, Ltd.
591 S. Mountain Rd.
New City, NY 10956
914-634-8832
800-MD-CREAM
Products: cosmetics, hypo-
allergenic skin care for men
and women, sun care
Availability: skin care clinics,
physicians, mail order
MO

Natracare
191 University Blvd.
Suite 294
Denver, CO 80206
303-320-1510
800-796-2872
www.indra.com/natracare
Products: feminine hygiene
Availability: drugstores,
health food stores,
supermarkets, cooperatives,
mail order
V MO

Natura
27134-A Paseo Espada
Suite 323
San Juan Capistrano, CA
92675
949-240-1104
800-933-1008
Products: aromatherapy,
fragrance for men and
women, hair oil, air
freshener, skin care for men
and women, essential oil,
massage oil
Availability: health food
stores, boutiques, specialty
stores, aromatherapists,
distributors, spas, mail order
V 🖾 MO

Naturade Cosmetics
7110 E. Jackson St.
Paramount, CA 90723
310-531-8120
800-421-1830
www.naturade.com
Products: baby care,
companion animal care,
cosmetics, hair care,
dandruff shampoo,
hypo-allergenic skin care for
men and women, toiletries
Availability: health food
stores, supermarkets,
cooperatives, boutiques,
specialty stores, mail order
🖾 MO

Natural (Surrey)
13110 Trails End Rd.
Leander, TX 78641
512-267-7172
Products: toiletries, shaving
supply, soap
Availability: drugstores,
department stores, health
food stores, supermarkets,
mail order
MO

**Natural Animal Health
Products, Inc.**
7000 U.S. 1 N.
St. Augustine, FL 32095
904-824-5884
800-274-7387
Products: companion animal
care, household supply, air
freshener, insect repellant
Availability: health food stores,
cooperatives, companion
animal supply stores,
veterinarians

Natural Bodycare
355 N. Lantana St.
Camarillo, CA 93010
805-445-9237
Products: aromatherapy,
fragrance for women, hair
care, dandruff shampoo,
skin care, sun care,
household supply, toiletries
Availability: health food
stores, mail order
V MO

Natural Chemistry
76 Progress Dr.
Stamford, CT 06902
203-316-4479
800-753-1233
Products: companion animal
care, household supply, pool
supply
Availability: health food
stores, cooperatives,
environmentally friendly
stores, mail order
MO

Naturally Yours, Alex
1848 Murray Ave.
Clearwater, FL 33755
813-443-7479
800-546-4164
Products: companion animal
care
Availability: health food
stores, companion animal
supply stores, holistic
veterinarians, mail order
V MO

Natural Products Company
7782 Newburg Rd.
Newburg, PA 17240-9601
717-423-5818
800-323-0418
Products: companion
animal care
Availability: health food
stores, companion animal
supply stores, gift stores
V

Natural Research People
South Route, Box 12
Lavina, MT 59046
406-575-4343
Products: companion
animal care
Availability: health food
stores, cooperatives,
companion animal supply
stores, veterinarians, mail
order
V MO

Natural Science
409 W. 76th St.
Davenport, IA 52806-1322
212-953-5200
888-EARTH-SAFE
Products: aromatherapy,
baby care, cosmetics,
fragrance for men and
women, hypo-allergenic
skin care for men and
women, sun care
Availability: drugstores,
department stores, health
food stores, mail order
V ★ MO

Natural World
6929 E. Greenway Pkwy.
Suite 100
Scottsdale, AZ 85254
602-905-1110
800-728-3388
Products: aromatherapy,
dental hygiene, hair care, air
freshener, car care, carpet
cleaning supply, furniture
polish, laundry detergent,
hypo-allergenic skin care,
sun care, toiletries, vitamins,
herbs
Availability: independent
sales representatives, mail
order
MO

**Nature Clean (Frank T. Ross
& Sons, Ltd.)**
6550 Lawrence Ave. E.
Scarborough, ON M1C 4A7
Canada
416-282-1107
Products: hair care,
household supply, bleach,
car care, carpet cleaning
supply, laundry detergent,
glue, soap
Availability: department
stores, drugstores, health
food stores, supermarkets,
cooperatives, mail order
V MO

**Nature de France, Ltd. (Para
Laboratories)**
100 Rose Ave.
Hempstead, NY 11550
516-538-4600
800-645-3752
www.queenhelene.com
Products: hair care, skin care
for women, toiletries, bathing
supply, deodorant, soap
Availability: department
stores, discount department
stores, drugstores, health
food stores, supermarkets,
cooperatives, boutiques,
specialty stores, mail order
V MO

Nature's Acres
8984 E. Weinke Rd.
North Freedom, WI 53951
608-522-4492
800-499-HERB
Products: aromatherapy,
baby care, companion
animal care, fragrance for
men and women, skin care
for men and women,
toiletries, bathing supply,
shaving supply, soap,
vitamins, herbs
Availability: health food
stores, boutiques, specialty
stores, mail order
MO

This Year, Millions Will Be Killed Because of What They're Wearing.

Most people don't realize the true cost of a fur. But the fact is, to make a single coat, dozens of animals must pay with their lives. Animals who are mercilessly trapped. Drowned. Even electrocuted or gassed on fur farms. So, if you're thinking about buying a fur – don't. Because, no matter what your reason is for wanting one, there are dozens of better reasons not to.

Don't Wear Fur.

 People for the Ethical Treatment of Animals
501 Front St., Norfolk, VA 23510 • 757-622-PETA
www.FurIsDead.com

Nature's Best (Natural Research People)
South Route, Box 12
Lavina, MT 59046
406-575-4343
Products: companion animal care
Availability: health food stores, companion animal supply stores, mail order
V MO

Nature's Country Pet
1765 Garnet Ave., Suite 12
San Diego, CA 92109
619-230-1058
800-576-PAWS
Products: companion animal care
Availability: health food stores, companion animal supply stores, mail order
V MO

Nature's Plus
548 Broadhollow Rd.
Melville, NY 11747-3708
516-293-0030
800-645-9500
Products: cosmetics, hair care, dandruff shampoo, nail care, skin care for men and women, toiletries, companion animal care, dietary supplements, Nature's Plus brand
Availability: health food stores

Nectarine
1011 Gilman St.
Berkeley, CA 94710
510-558-7100
800-966-3457
Products: fragrance for men and women, hair care, nail care, skin care for men and women, toiletries, bathing supply, shaving supply, soap
Availability: boutiques, specialty stores

Neocare Laboratories
33 Journey, Suite 200
Aliso Viejo, CA 92656
714-360-1193
Products: hypo-allergenic skin care for men and women, household supply, pool and spa supply, odor eliminator, grease trap and septic tank control supply
Availability: health food stores, cooperatives, mail order
V MO

Neo Soma
P.O. Box 50933
Eugene, OR 97405
541-431-3359
Products: hair care, skin care
Availability: health clubs, country clubs, pro shops, sporting goods stores
V

New Age Products
16200 N. Hwy. 101
Willits, CA 95490-9710
707-459-5969
888-7-NEW-AGE
Products: biodegradable household detergent
Availability: health food stores, cooperatives
V

Neway
Little Harbor
42 Doaks La.
Marblehead, MA 01945
617-631-9400
Products: household supply
Availability: health food stores, mail order
V MO

Neways
150 E. 400 N.
Salem, UT 84653
801-423-2800
800-998-7233
Products: cosmetics, dental hygiene, hair care, hypo-allergenic skin care for men and women, sun care, household supply, nail care, toiletries, shaving supply
Availability: boutiques, specialty stores, distributors, mail order
MO

New Chapter Extracts
99 Main St.
P.O. Box 1947
Brattleboro, VT 05301
802-257-0018
800-543-7279
www.newchapter.com
Products: skin care, nutritional supplements, herbal extracts, ginger delivery system
Availability: health food stores, cooperatives, physicians, aestheticians, mail order
V MO

Nexxus Products Company
82 Coromar Dr.
Santa Barbara, CA 93116
805-968-6900
www.nexxusproducts.com
Products: hair care, dandruff shampoo, hair color, permanents, toiletries, vitamins
Availability: salons

Nikken
15363 Varrance Pkwy.
Irvine, CA 92618
949-789-2000
Products: skin care

Nirvana
P.O. Box 26275
Minneapolis, MN 55426
612-932-2919
800-432-2919
Products: aromatherapy, hair
care, skin care
Availability: drugstores,
health food stores, cooperatives, mail order

Nivea (Beiersdorf)
BDF Plaza
360 Martin Luther King Dr.
Norwalk, CT 06856-5529
203-853-8008
Products: skin care
Availability: drugstores,
supermarkets

No Common Scents
Kings Yard
220 Xenia Ave.
Yellow Springs, OH 45387
937-767-4261
800-686-0012
Products: fragrance for men
and women, air freshener,
companion animal care,
incense, bath crystals
Availability: No Common
Scents store, mail order
MO

Nordstrom
865 Market St.
San Francisco, CA 94103
800-7-BEAUTY
Products: Single Notes
(fragrance), Simple and
Natural Essentials (skin care
and makeup), Nordstrom
Essentials (bathing supply),
Nordstrom Bath Ltd. (bathing
supply)
Availability: Nordstrom
department stores, mail order
MO

Norelco
1010 Washington Blvd.
P.O. Box 120015
Stamford, CT 06912-0015
203-973-0200
Products: electric razors
Availability: department
stores, drugstores, super-
markets
V

**North Country Glycerine
Soap**
7888 County Rd., #6
Maple Plain, MN 55359
612-479-3381
800-667-1202
www.pclink.com/nocosoap/
Products: baby care,
companion animal care,
ethnic personal care, hair
care, insect repellant,
hypo-allergenic skin care,
sun care, bathing supply,
deodorant, soap
Availability: department
stores, drugstores, health
food stores, boutiques,
specialty stores, companion
animal supply stores, sports
supply stores, mail order
MO

N/R Laboratories, Inc.
900 E. Franklin St.
Centerville, OH 45459
513-433-9570
800-223-9348
Products: companion animal
care
Availability: distributors,
mail order
MO

NuSkin International
One NuSkin Plaza
75 W. Center
Provo, UT 84601
801-377-6056
800-366-6875
www.nuskin.com
Products: hair care, skin care
for men and women, sun
care, toiletries, nutritional
supplements
Availability: distributors,
mail order
MO

NutriBiotic
865 Parallel Dr.
Lakeport, CA 95453
707-263-0411
800-225-4345
Products: dental hygiene,
toiletries, nutritional
supplements
Availability: health food
stores

Nutri-Cell (Derma-Glo)
1038 N. Tustin, Suite 309
Orange, CA 92667-5958
714-953-8307
Products: skin care,
vitamins, herbs
Availability: health food
stores, mail order

Nutri-Metics International
3915 61st Ave. S.E.
Calgary AB T2C 1V5
Canada
800-267-7546
Products: cosmetics,
toiletries, household supply
Availability: distributors,
mail order
MO

NATURAL OLIVE OIL SOAP

ABEA ®

from the...
Mediterranean Island of Crete

OLIVA LIMITED
P.O. BOX #4387
READING, PA 19606
610-779-7854

The Ohio Hempery
7002 S.R. 329
Guysville, OH 45735
614-662-4367
800-BUY-HEMP
www.hempery.com
Products: cosmetics, skin
care, clothing, hemp
Availability: health food
stores, mail order
MO

Oliva Ltd.
P.O. Box 4387
Reading, PA 19606
610-779-7854
Products: soap
Availability: health food
stores, mail order
V MO

OPI Products
13034 Saticoy St.
N. Hollywood, CA 91605
818-759-2400
800-341-9999
Products: nail care
Availability: beauty supply
stores, salons

Orange-Mate
P.O. Box 883
Waldport, OR 97394
503-563-3290
800-626-8685
Products: air freshener
Availability: department
stores, discount department
stores, drugstores, health food
stores, cooperatives, specialty
stores, independent sales
representatives, mail order
V MO

Oriflame USA
8300 W. Flagler St.
Suite 210
Miami, FL 33144-2096
305-463-4688
Products: cosmetics,
fragrance for men and
women, hair care, hypo-
allergenic skin care for men
and women, sun care,
toiletries, vitamins
Availability: distributors,
mail order
MO

**Origins Natural Resources
(Estée Lauder)**
767 Fifth Ave.
New York, NY 10153
212-572-4100
Products: cosmetics, vegan
makeup brushes, ethnic
personal care, fragrance,
skin care, sun care,
toiletries, bathing supply,
shaving supply, soap,
sensory therapy
Availability: department
stores, Origins stores,
boutiques, specialty stores

Orjene Natural Cosmetics
5-43 48th Ave.
Long Island City, NY 11101
718-937-2666
800-886-7536
Products: cosmetics, hair
care, skin care for men and
women, sun care, toiletries,
shaving supply
Availability: health food
stores, cooperatives, mail
order
MO

Orlane
555 Madison Ave.
New York, NY 10022
212-750-1111
800-535-3628
Products: cosmetics,
fragrance for women, nail
care, hypo-allergenic skin
care for women, sun care
Availability: department
stores, boutiques, specialty
stores

Orly International
9309 Deering Ave.
Chatsworth, CA 91311
818-998-1111
800-275-1111
www.orlyproducts.com
Products: nail care
Availability: discount
department stores, drugstores

Otto Basics—Beauty 2 Go!
P.O. Box 9023
Rancho Santa Fe, CA 92067
619-756-2026
800-598-OTTO
Products: cosmetics
Availability: department
stores, QVC, direct TV
marketing, mail order
MO

Oxyfresh Worldwide
E. 12928 Indiana Ave.
P.O. Box 3723
Spokane, WA 99220
509-924-4999
Products: companion animal
care, dental hygiene,
toothbrushes, hair care,
household supply, air
freshener, laundry detergent,
skin care for men and
women, toiletries, bathing
supply, soap, vitamins
Availability: independent
sales representatives, mail
order
V **MO**

Pacific Scents
P.O. Box 8205
Calabasas, CA 91375-8205
818-999-0832
800-554-7236
Products: toiletries,
audiocassettes with
subliminal affirmations,
essential oil
Availability: health food
stores, mail order
V **MO**

Parlux Fragrances
3725 S.W. 30th Ave.
Ft. Lauderdale, FL 33312
954-316-9008
800-727-5895
Products: cosmetics,
fragrance for men and
women
Availability: department
stores, drugstores, boutiques,
specialty stores
V

Pathmark Stores
301 Blair Rd.
Woodbridge, NJ 07095
908-499-3000
Products: dental hygiene,
toothbrushes, air freshener,
baking soda, razors,
vitamins
Availability: Pathmark
supermarkets and drug-
stores in Conn., N.J., N.Y.,
Pa., Del.

**Patricia Allison Natural
Beauty Products**
4470 Monahan Rd.
La Mesa, CA 91941
619-444-4163
800-858-8742
Products: cosmetics,
fragrance for women, hair
care, hypo-allergenic skin
care for men and women,
sun care, toiletries, bathing
supply
Availability: mail order
MO

Paul Mazzotta
P.O. Box 96
Reading, PA 19607
610-376-2250
800-562-1357
Products: cosmetics, hair care, dandruff shampoo, hair color, permanents, hypo-allergenic skin care for men and women, sun care, toiletries
Availability: salons, Paul Mazzotta stores, mail order

Paul Mitchell
9701 Wilshire Blvd.
Suite 1205
Beverly Hills, CA 90212
310-248-3888
800-321-JPMS
Products: hair care, skin care, sun care
Availability: salons

Perfect Balance Cosmetics
2 Ridgewood Rd.
Malvern, PA 19355-9629
610-647-7780
Products: cosmetics, fragrance for men and women, hair care, hypo-allergenic skin care for men and women, sun care, thigh-smoothing cream
Availability: independent sales representatives, distributors, health clubs, spas, salons, mail order
MO

The Pet Connection
P.O. Box 391806
Mountain View, CA 94039
650-596-9933
www.royalherbal.com
Products: companion animal care, carpet cleaning supply
Availability: health food stores, boutiques, specialty stores, mail order
MO

PetGuard
165 Industrial Loop S.
Unit 5
Orange Park, FL 32073
904-264-8500
800-874-3221
Products: companion animal care
Availability: health food stores, cooperatives, companion animal supply stores, environmentally friendly stores, veterinarians

Pets 'n People (Nature's Miracle)
27520 Hawthorne Blvd.
Suite 215
Rolling Hills Estates, CA 90274
310-544-7125
Products: companion animal cleaning supply, carpet cleaning supply, litter treatment, Nature's Miracle
Availability: companion animal supply stores, mail order
V MO

Pharmagel International
P.O. Box 2288
Monterey, CA 93942
831-649-2300
800-882-4889
Products: hypo-allergenic skin care for men and women
Availability: health food stores, boutiques, specialty stores, salons, mail order
V MO

Pierre Fabré
1055 W. Eighth St.
Azusa, CA 91702
818-334-3395
Products: cosmetics, hypo-allergenic skin care, sun care
Availability: drugstores

Pilot Corporation of America
60 Commerce Dr.
Trumbull, CT 06611
203-377-8800
www.pilotpen.com
Products: office supply, writing instruments
Availability: drugstores, supermarkets, office supply stores, catalogs

Planet
P.O. Box 48184
Victoria, BC V8Z 7H6
Canada
800-858-8449
www.planetinc.com
Products: household supply, laundry detergent, dish detergent, all-purpose cleaner
Availability: health food stores, supermarkets, cooperatives, mail order

PlantEssence Natural Body Care
P.O. Box 14743
Portland, OR 97293-0743
503-281-4147
800-752-6898
Products: fragrance for men and women, skin care for men and women, air freshener, toiletries, body oil, lip balm, breath freshener
Availability: health food stores, cooperatives, boutiques, specialty stores, mail order
MO

Prescription Plus Clinical Skin Care
25028 Kearny Ave.
Valencia, CA 91355
800-877-4849
Products: skin care for men and women, sun care
Availability: professional skin care salons and clinics, day spas, physicians

Prescriptives (Estée Lauder)
767 Fifth Ave.
New York, NY 10153
212-572-4400
Products: cosmetics, ethnic personal care, fragrance for women, skin care, sun care, toiletries, bathing supply, soap
Availability: department stores, specialty stores

Prestige Cosmetics
1441 W. Newport Center Dr.
Deerfield Beach, FL 33442
305-480-9202
800-722-7488
Products: cosmetics, nail care
Availability: drugstores, supermarkets, boutiques, specialty stores, beauty supply stores

Prestige Fragrances Ltd. (Revlon)
625 Madison Ave.
New York, NY 10022
212-572-5000
Products: fragrance for women
Availability: department stores

The Principal Secret
41-550 Ecclectic St., Suite 200
Palm Desert, CA 92260
800-545-5595
Products: skin care for men and women
Availability: J.C. Penney, home shopping networks, mail order
MO

Professional Pet Products
1873 N.W. 97th Ave.
Miami, FL 33172
305-592-1992
800-432-5349
Products: companion animal care
Availability: drugstores, cooperatives, companion animal supply stores, mail order
MO

Pro-Tec Pet Health
5440 Camus Rd.
Carson City, NV 89701-9306
775-884-2566
800-44-FLEAS
www.protec-pet-health.com
Products: companion animal care
Availability: health food stores, companion animal supply stores, mail order
★ MO

Pulse Products
2021 Ocean Ave., #105
Santa Monica, CA 90405
310-399-3447
310-392-0991
Products: massage oil
Availability: health food stores, mail order
V MO

Pure & Basic Products
20600 Belshaw Ave.
Carson, CA 90746
310-898-1630
800-432-3787
www.pureandbasic.com
Products: hair care, dandruff shampoo, household supply, air freshener, hypo-allergenic skin care for men and women, toiletries, bathing supply, deodorant, shaving supply, soap
Availability: cooperatives, beauty supply stores, salons, mail order
V ⬛ MO

Pure Touch Therapeutic Body Care
P.O. Box 1281
Nevada City, CA 95959
800-442-7873
Products: fragrance for women, spa supply for massage professionals
Availability: health food stores, spas, distributors, mail order
V MO

Quan Yin Essentials
5333 Dry Creek Rd.
Healdsburg, CA 95448
707-431-0529
Products: fragrance for men and women, skin care for men and women, toiletries
Availability: department stores, health food stores, boutiques, specialty stores, gift stores, independent sales representatives, mail order
V MO

Queen Helene
100 Rose Ave.
Hempstead, NY 11550
516-538-4600
800-645-3752
www.queenhelene.com
Products: hair care, skin care
for women, toiletries,
bathing supply, deodorant,
soap
Availability: department
stores, discount department
stores, drugstores, health
food stores, supermarkets,
cooperatives, boutiques,
specialty stores, mail order
MO

Rachel Perry
9800 Eton Ave.
Chatsworth, CA 91311
818-886-0202
800-966-8888
www.rachelperry.net
Products: skin care, sun care
Availability: drugstores,
health food stores, supermarkets, mail order
⭐ MO

Rainbow Research Corp.
170 Wilbur Place
Bohemia, NY 11716
516-589-5563
800-722-9595
www.rainbowresearch.com
Products: baby care, hair
care, hair color,
hypo-allergenic skin care for
men and women, bathing
supply, soap, massage oil
Availability: drugstores,
health food stores,
supermarkets, cooperatives,
boutiques, specialty stores,
mail order
MO

The Rainforest Company
701 N. 15th St., Suite 500
St. Louis, MO 63103
314-621-1330
www.the-rainforest-co.com
Products: aromatherapy, hair
care, toiletries, bathing
supply, soap, rain
forest-derived gifts
Availability: health food
stores, boutiques, specialty
stores

**Ralph Lauren Fragrances
(Cosmair)**
575 Fifth Ave.
New York, NY 10017
212-818-1500
Products: fragrance
Availability: department
stores

Real Animal Friends
101 Albany Ave.
Freeport, NY 11520
516-223-7600
Products: companion
animal care
Availability: discount
department stores,
boutiques, specialty stores,
companion animal supply
stores, mail order

Redken Laboratories
575 Fifth Ave.
New York, NY 10017
212-818-1500
800-423-5369
Products: cosmetics,
fragrance for women, hair
care, dandruff shampoo, hair
color, permanents,
hypo-allergenic skin care for
men and women, toiletries,
shaving supply
Availability: salons

Rejuvi Skin Care
212 Michelle Ct.
S. San Francisco, CA
94080
650-588-7794
www.dalnet.se/~rejuvi
Products: hair care, skin care
Availability: salons, spas,
dermatologists, mail order
⭐ MO

Reviva Labs
705 Hopkins Rd.
Haddonfield, NJ 08033
609-428-3885
800-257-7774
Products: baby care,
cosmetics, hair care,
dandruff shampoo,
hypo-allergenic skin care for
men and women, sun care,
toiletries, shaving supply
Availability: discount
department stores,
drugstores, health food
stores, supermarkets,
cooperatives, boutiques,
distributors, mail order
MO

Revlon
625 Madison Ave.
New York, NY 10022
212-572-5000
800-473-8566
www.revlon.com
Products: cosmetics, ethnic
personal care, hair care, hair
color, nail care, toiletries,
deodorant, Almay, Flex, Jean
Naté, Outrageous, Ultima II
Availability: discount
department stores,
department stores,
drugstores, supermarkets,
beauty supply stores

Rivers Run
6120 W. Tropicana A16-357
Las Vegas, NV 89103
702-252-3477
800-560-6753
www.riversrun.qpg.com
Products: companion animal care, car care, carpet cleaning supply, laundry detergent, oven cleaner, hypo-allergenic skin care for men and women, all-purpose cleaner, graffiti remover
Availability: Rivers Run stores, mail order
V MO

Royal Labs Natural Cosmetics
Box 22434
Charleston, SC 29413
803-552-1504
800-760-7779
Products: aromatherapy, chemical-free cosmetics, hair care, hypo-allergenic skin care for men and women, sun care, toiletries, bathing supply, shaving supply
Availability: health food stores, supermarkets, boutiques, specialty stores, skin clinics, salons, spas, mail order
V MO

Rusk
One Cummings Point Rd.
Stamford, CT 06904
203-316-4300
800-829-7875
www.rusk1.com
Products: hair care
Availability: salons

Sacred Blends
P.O. Box 634
Applegate, CA 95703
530-878-7464
888-722-7331
www.jps.net/sacred1
Products: baby care, skin care for men and women, herbs
Availability: health food stores, cooperatives, mail order, Web site
★ MO

Safeway
5918 Stoneridge Mall Rd.
Pleasanton, CA 94588-3229
510-467-3000
Products: baby care, toothbrushes, household supply, toiletries,
Availability: Safeway supermarkets

Sagami
825 N. Cass Ave., Suite 101
Westmont, IL 60559
630-789-9999
Products: condoms
(Excalibur, Sagami Type E,
Vis-à-Vis, Peace & Sound
regular, Peace & Sound ultra
thin)
Availability: drugstores,
supermarkets, specialty
stores

Sanford
2711 Washington Blvd.
Bellwood, IL 60104
708-547-5525
800-323-0749
www.sanfordcorp.com
Products: office supply, ink,
writing instruments
Availability: department
stores, drugstores,
supermarkets, office supply
stores, mail order
MO

**Santa Fe Botanical
Fragrances**
P.O. Box 282
Santa Fe, NM 87504
505-473-1717
Products: aromatherapy,
fragrance for men and
women, botanical colognes
Availability: natural food
stores, mail order
V MO

The Santa Fe Soap Company
369 Montezuma, #167
Santa Fe, NM 87501
505-986-6064
888-SOAP-BAR
Products: hair care,
toiletries, soap
Availability: department
stores, health food stores,
supermarkets, cooperatives,
boutiques, specialty stores,
independent sales
representatives, bath shops,
mail order

Sappo Hill Soapworks
654 Tolman Creek Rd.
Ashland, OR 97520
541-482-4485
Products: soap
Availability: health food
stores

Sassaby (Jane, Estée Lauder)
767 Fifth Ave.
New York, NY 10153
212-572-4200
Products: cosmetics
Availability: drugstores

The air in our homes is 2 to 5 times more polluted than the air outside.

Environmental Protection Agency 4/8/99

Traditional household cleaning products contain a multitude of toxic chemicals that can endanger your health and pollute the air in your home

·SEVENTH· GENERATION®

Safer for you and the environment
www.seventhgen.com
A complete line of non-toxic household products

Schiff Products
1960 S. 4250 W.
Salt Lake City, UT 84104
801-972-0300
800-444-5200
Products: vitamin and
mineral supplements
Availability: health food
stores, mail order

Scruples
8231 214th St. W.
Lakeville, MN 55044
612-469-4646
800-457-0016
www.scrupleshaircare.com
Products: hair care, hair
color, permanents
Availability: salons

Sea-renity
c/o Israel Business Centers
Tel-Aviv Hilton
Independence Park
Tel-Aviv, Israel 63405
972-3-520-22
Products: aromatherapy, skin
and spa care for men and
women, soap, bath salts, Dead
Sea black mud body wraps,
holistic scrubs, shower gel
Availability: health food
stores, cooperatives,
boutiques, specialty stores,
distributors, mail order
MO

Sebastian International
P.O. Box 4111
Woodland Hills, CA 91365
818-999-5112
800-829-7322
Products: hair care, hair
color, skin care for women
Availability: salons, Sebastian
collective salon members

SerVaas Laboratories
P.O. Box 7008
1200 Waterway Blvd.
Indianapolis, IN 46207
317-636-7760
800-433-5818
Products: household supply
Availability: discount
department stores,
drugstores, supermarkets
V

Seventh Generation
One Mill St., Suite A-26
Burlington, VT 05401-1530
802-658-3773
800-456-1177
Products: baby care,
feminine hygiene, house-
hold supply, nonchlorine
bleach, laundry detergent,
dish detergent, 100%
recycled paper products
Availability: health food
stores, supermarkets,
cooperatives, mail order
V ✪ ❀ MO

Shadow Lake
P.O. Box 2597
Danbury, CT 06813-2597
203-778-0881
800-343-6588
Products: aromatherapy,
baby care, household
supply, air freshener, car
care, carpet cleaning supply,
oven cleaner, toiletries,
bathing supply, soap
Availability: discount
department stores, health
food stores, supermarkets,
cooperatives, boutiques,
specialty stores, mail order
V MO

Shahin Soap Company
427 Van Dyke Ave.
Haledon, NJ 07508
201-790-4296
Products: soap
Availability: mail order
V MO

Shaklee Corporation
444 Market St.
San Francisco, CA 94111
415-954-3000
800-SHAKLEE
www.shaklee.com
Products: baby care,
cosmetics, dental hygiene,
fragrance, hair care, laundry
detergent, hypo-allergenic
skin care, sun care,
toiletries, bathing supply,
deodorant, shaving supply,
soap, vitamins, herbs
Availability: independent
sales representatives

Shikai (Trans-India Products)
P.O. Box 2866
Santa Rosa, CA 95405
707-544-0298
800-448-0298
www.shikai.com
Products: hair care, hair
color, skin care for men and
women, toiletries, bathing
supply, facial care, hand and
body lotion
Availability: drugstores,
health food stores,
supermarkets, cooperatives,
boutiques, specialty stores,
mail order
MO

Shirley Price Aromatherapy
P.O. Box 65
Pineville, PA 18946
215-598-3802
Products: hypo-allergenic
skin care for men and
women, pure essential oil of
therapeutic quality
Availability: health food
stores, massage therapists,
salons, spas, mail order
★ MO

**Shivani Ayurvedic
Cosmetics (Devi)**
P.O. Box 377
Lancaster, MA 01523
508-368-0066
800-237-8221
Products: aromatherapy,
cosmetics, fragrance, hair
care, skin care, toiletries,
bathing supply, deodorant,
shaving supply, soap
Availability: health food
stores, cooperatives,
boutiques, specialty stores,
independent sales
representatives, mail order
MO

**Simplers Botanical
Company**
P.O. Box 39
6450 First St.
Forestville, CA 95436
707-887-7570
800-6-JASMIN
Products: aromatherapy,
companion animal care,
personal care, herbal
extracts, Sierra Sage Salves
Availability: health food
stores, mail order

Simple Wisdom
775 S. Graham
Memphis, TN 38111
901-458-4686
Products: fragrance, hair
care, household supply,
all-purpose cleaner, carpet
cleaning supply, laundry
detergent, spot remover, skin
care, toiletries, liquid soap,
bathing supply, massage oil
Availability: drugstores,
health food stores,
cooperatives, mail order
MO

Sinclair & Valentine
480 Airport Blvd.
Watsonville, CA 95076-
2056
831-722-9526
800-722-1434
Products: aromatherapy,
fragrance for women,
household supply, air
freshener, skin care for
women, toiletries, bathing
supply, shaving supply, soap,
foot care, massage oil
Availability: discount
department stores,
drugstores, supermarkets,
independent sales
representatives

Sirena
P.O. Box 112220
Carrollton, TX 75011
214-357-1464
800-527-2368
Products: Sirena liquid and bar soaps
Availability: health food stores, mail order
V MO

Smith & Vandiver
480 Airport Blvd.
Watsonville, CA 95076-2056
831-722-9526
800-722-1434
www.fizzmos.com
Products: aromatherapy, baby care, fragrance for women, household supply, air freshener, nail care, skin care for men and women, toiletries, bathing supply, shaving supply, soap, foot care, massage oil
Availability: department stores, health food stores, boutiques, specialty stores, independent sales representatives

The Soap Opera
319 State St.
Madison, WI 53703
608-251-4051
800-251-7627
www.thesoapopera.com
Products: aromatherapy, toothbrushes, fragrance, hair care, hair color, personal care, deodorant
Availability: The Soap Opera store, mail order
V ★ MO

Legend

V — Vegan (products contain no animal ingredients)

★ — Company meets CSCA

▨ — Company uses Caring Consumer product logo

MO — Mail order available

Sojourner Farms Natural Pet Products
1 - 19th Ave. S.
Minneapolis, MN 55454
612-343-7262
888-867-6567
www.sojos.com
Products: companion animal care, food, and supply
Availability: health food stores, supermarkets, cooperatives, specialty stores, mail order
MO

Solgar Vitamin Company
500 Willow Tree Rd.
Leonia, NJ 07605
201-944-2311
www.solgar.com
Products: vitamins
Availability: health food stores, cooperatives

Sombra Cosmetics
5600-G McLeod N.E.
Albuquerque, NM 87109
505-888-0288
800-225-3963
Products: cosmetics, skin care, theatrical makeup
Availability: health food stores, mail order
MO

Sonoma Soap Company
P.O. Box 750428
Petaluma, CA 94975-0428
707-769-5120
www.avalonproducts.net
Products: hypo-allergenic skin care, toiletries, bathing supply, soap
Availability: health food stores, boutiques, specialty stores
MO

SoRik International
278 Taileyand Ave.
Jacksonville, FL 32202
904-353-4200
800-824-8255
Products: hair care, sun care, toiletries
Availability: salons
MO

Soya System
10441 Midwest Industrial
St. Louis, MO 63132
314-428-0004
www.soya.com
Products: hair care, permanents
Availability: beauty supply stores, salons

Spa Natural Beauty Products
P.O. Box 31473
Aurora, CO 80041
800-598-3878
Products: cosmetics, fragrance for women, hair care, hypo-allergenic skin care for men and women, sun care, toiletries
Availability: Spa Natural Beauty Products stores, mail order
MO

Staedtler, Ltd.
Cowbridge Rd.
Pontyclym, Mid Glamorgan
Wales, Great Britain
0448 237421
Products: office supply, writing instruments
Availability: office supply stores in the U.K.

Stanhome
50 Payson Ave.
Easthampton, MA 01027-2262
413-527-4001
Products: household supply
Availability: hardware stores, distributors

Steps in Health, Ltd.
P.O. Box 1409
Lake Grove, NY 11755
516-471-2432
800-471-8343
Products: companion animal care, dental hygiene, hair care, household supply, air freshener, skin care for women, toiletries, deodorant, soap, vitamins
Availability: mail order
MO

Stevens Research Salon Products
19417 63rd Ave. N.E.
Arlington, WA 98223
360-435-4513
800-262-3344
Products: hair care, permanents
Availability: salons, beauty schools
V

Studio Magic Cosmetics
20135 Cypress Creek Dr.
Alva, FL 33920-3305
941-728-3344
800-452-7706
Products: baby care, cosmetics, hypo-allergenic skin care, sun care, theatrical makeup, vitamins, herbs
Availability: boutiques, specialty stores, independent sales representatives, physicians, spas, mail order
MO

Sukesha
P.O. Box 5126
Manchester, NH 03108
603-669-4228
800-221-3496
Products: hair care, hair color, permanents
Availability: salons

Sumeru
P.O. Box 1008
Silver Lake, WI 53170
800-478-6378
www.internatural.com
Products: aromatherapy, baby care, personal care
Availability: health food stores, mail order
V **MO**

SunFeather Natural Soap Company
1551 Hwy. 72
Potsdam, NY 13676
315-265-3648
800-771-7627
www.electroniccottage.com/sunfeathersoaps/
Products: aromatherapy, baby care, companion animal care, shampoo bars, insect repellant, soap-making supply, personal care, modeling soap for children
Availability: department stores, drugstores, health food stores, cooperatives, boutiques, specialty stores, independent sales representatives, mail order
V **⬛** **MO**

Sunrider International
1625 Abalone Ave.
Torrance, CA 90501
310-781-3808
Products: cosmetics, dental hygiene, fragrance, hair care, household supply, nail care, skin care, sun care, toiletries, bathing supply, shaving supply, soap, vitamins
Availability: independent sales representatives

	Legend
V	Vegan (products contain no animal ingredients)
★	Company meets CSCA
⬛	Company uses Caring Consumer product logo
MO	Mail order available

Sunrise Lane
780 Greenwich St., Dept. PT
New York, NY 10014
212-242-7014
Products: baby care, dental
hygiene, hair care, hair
color, permanents, bleach,
carpet cleaning supply,
laundry detergent, hypo-
allergenic skin care, bathing
supply, deodorant, shaving
supply, soap
Availability: mail order
MO

Sunshine Natural Products
Rte. 5P
Renick, WV 24966
304-497-3163
Products: companion
animal care, hair care,
dandruff shampoo
Availability: health food
stores, cooperatives, mail
order

Sunshine Products Group
2545-A Prairie Rd.
Eugene, OR 97402
503-461-2160
800-285-6457
Products: aromatherapy,
essential oil, herbal oil,
body lotion, massage oil
Availability: drugstores,
health food stores, mail
order

**Supreme Beauty Products
Company**
820 S. Michigan
Chicago, IL 60605
312-322-0670
800-272-6602
Products: hair care
Availability: drugstores, mail
order
MO

Surrey
13110 Trails End Rd.
Leander, TX 78641
512-267-7172
Products: toiletries, shaving
supply
Availability: department
stores, discount department
stores, drugstores, health
food stores, supermarkets,
distributors

Tammy Taylor Nails
18007E Skypark Cir.
Irvine, CA 92714
714-756-6606
800-748-6665
Products: cosmetics, nail care,
skin care, hypo-allergenic
skin care, sun care, toiletries
Availability: Tammy Taylor
stores, distributors, mail order
MO

TaUT by Leonard Engelman
9424 Eton Ave., Unit H
Chatsworth, CA 91311
818-773-3975
800-438-8288
www.tautcosmetics.com
Products: cosmetics,
hypo-allergenic skin care for
men and women, sun care,
theatrical makeup
Availability: health food
stores, boutiques, specialty
stores, beauty supply stores,
salons, mail order
MO

Terra Nova
1011 Gilman St.
Berkeley, CA 94710
510-558-7100
www.terranovabody.com
Products: fragrance for
women, toiletries, bathing
supply, soap
Availability: department
stores, boutiques, specialty
stores

Terressentials
2650 Old National Pike
Middletown, MD 21769-8817
301-371-7333
Products: cosmetics,
fragrance for men and
women, hair care, hair color,
household supply, air
freshener, insect repellant, skin
care, bathing supply,
deodorant, shaving supply,
soap, vitamins, herbs
Availability: health food
stores, Terressentials stores,
boutiques, specialty stores,
mail order
V MO

Thursday Plantation
P.O. Box 5613
Santa Barbara, CA 93150-
5613
805-963-2297
800-645-9500
Products: dental hygiene,
hair care, dandruff shampoo,
hypo-allergenic skin care for
men and women, sun care,
toiletries
Availability: drugstores,
health food stores,
supermarkets

**Tish & Snooky's (Manic
Panic)**
64-66 White St., 3rd Fl.
New York, NY 10013
212-941-0656
800-95-MANIC
Products: cosmetics, hair
bleach, hair color, nail care
Availability: department
stores, drugstores, health
food stores, mail order
MO

Tisserand Aromatherapy
P.O. Box 750428
Petaluma, CA 94975-0428
707-769-5120
www.avalonproducts.net
Products: aromatherapy, hair
care, hypo-allergenic skin
care, toiletries, bathing
supply, soap
Availability: department
stores, health food stores,
boutiques, specialty stores,
salons, spas, mail order
V MO

Tom's of Maine
P.O. Box 710
302 Lafayette Ctr.
Kennebunk, ME 04043
207-985-2944
800-367-8667
www.toms-of-maine.com
Products: baby care, dental
hygiene, hair care, toiletries,
deodorant, shaving supply,
soap
Availability: drugstores,
health food stores,
supermarkets, cooperatives,
Tom's of Maine stores,
boutiques, specialty stores,
mail order
★ MO

Tova Corporation
192 N. Canon Dr.
Beverly Hills, CA 90210
310-246-0218
Products: fragrance, hair
care, skin care
Availability: department
stores, boutiques, QVC

Trader Joe's Company
P.O. Box 3270
538 Mission St.
South Pasadena, CA 91030
818-441-1177
Products: hair care,
household supply, toiletries
Availability: Trader Joe's
Company stores

Travel Mates America
23750 St. Clair Ave.
Cleveland, OH 44117
216-738-2222
Products: hair care, toiletries
Availability: private label for
hotel industry only

Tressa
P.O. Box 75320
Cincinnati, OH 45275
606-525-1300
800-879-8737
Products: hair care
Availability: salons

TRI Hair Care Products
13918 Equitable Rd.
Cerritos, CA 90703
562-494-6300
800-458-8874
www.trihaircare.com
Products: hair care
Availability: boutiques,
specialty stores, mail order
MO

Trophy Animal Health Care
2796 Helen St.
Pensacola, FL 32504
850-476-7087
800-336-7087
Products: companion animal
care
Availability: cooperatives,
mail order
MO

Tropix Suncare Products
1014 Laurel St., Suite 200
Brainerd, MN 56401-3779
800-421-7314
Products: sun care
Availability: tanning salons
V

Truly Moist
74-940 Hwy. 111, Suite 437
Indian Wells, CA 92201
619-346-1604
800-243-4435
Products: hypo-allergenic
skin care for men and
women
Availability: drugstores,
health food stores

Tyra Skin Care for Men and
Women
9424 Eaton Ave., Suite J
Chatsworth, CA 91311
818-407-1274
Products: hypo-allergenic
skin care for men and
women, sun care
Availability: department
stores, boutiques, specialty
stores, mail order
MO

The Ultimate Life
P.O. Box 4308
Santa Barbara, CA 93140
805-962-2221
800-843-6325
www.ultimatelife.com
Products: vitamins, herbs,
nutritional powder, mealbars
Availability: health food
stores, health care
practitioners, mail order
V 🕭 MO

Ultima II (Revlon)
625 Madison Ave.
New York, NY 10022
212-572-5000
Products: cosmetics
Availability: department
stores

Ultra Glow Cosmetics (Nickull-Dowdall)
P.O. Box 1469, Station A
Vancouver, BC V6C 2P7
Canada
604-939-3329
Products: cosmetics, sun care, theatrical makeup
Availability: department stores, drugstores, boutiques, specialty stores, mail order
V MO

Un-petroleum Lip Care
P.O. Box 750428
Petaluma, CA 94975-0428
707-769-5120
www.avalonproducts.net
Products: lip care
Availability: health food stores, mail order
MO

Upper Canada Soap & Candle Makers
1510 Caterpillar Rd.
Mississauga, ON L4X 2W9
Canada
905-897-1710
Products: toiletries, soap, candles
Availability: gift stores

Urban Decay
345 California St., Suite 3300
San Francisco, CA 94104
650-988-9969
800-784-URBAN
www.urbandecay.com
Products: cosmetics, hair color, nail care, theatrical makeup
Availability: discount department stores, boutiques, specialty stores, mail order
★ MO

USA King's Crossing
P.O. Box 832074
Richardson, TX 75083
972-801-9473
800-SHAV-KING
www.shaveking.com
Products: razors, blades, skin care for men and women, shaving supply
Availability: drugstores, health food stores, specialty stores, mail order
V ▨ MO

U.S. Sales Service (Crystal Orchid)
374 W. Citation
Tempe, AZ 85284
602-839-3761
800-487-2633
Products: deodorant stones, soap
Availability: health food stores, cooperatives, independent sales representatives, mail order
V ▨ MO

Vapor Products
P.O. Box 568395
Orlando, FL 32856-8395
407-851-6230
800-621-2943
Products: household supply, mold and mildew prevention
Availability: discount department stores, supermarkets, Home Depot, mail order
MO

Vermont Soapworks
616 Exchange St.
Middlebury, VT 05753
802-388-4302
www.vermontsoap.com
Products: aromatherapy, baby care, household supply, air freshener, carpet cleaning supply, laundry supply for fine washables, hypo-allergenic skin care, soap, nontoxic cleaner, fruit and veggie wash
Availability: department stores, drugstores, health food stores, cooperatives, Vermont Soapworks stores, boutiques, specialty stores, mail order
MO

Veterinarian's Best
P.O. Box 4459
Santa Barbara, CA 93103
805-963-5609
800-866-PETS
www.vetsbest.com
Products: companion animal care
Availability: health food stores, supermarkets, specialty stores, companion animal supply stores, mail order
V MO

Victoria's Secret
4 Limited Pkwy.
Reynoldsburg, OH 43068
614-577-7111
www.limited.com
Products: fragrance and skin care for women, sun care, toiletries
Availability: Victoria's Secret stores, mail order
MO

Legend

V   Vegan (products contain no animal ingredients)

★   Company meets CSCA

☒   Company uses Caring Consumer product logo

MO   Mail order available

Virginia's Soap, Ltd.
Module 1, Compartment 9
Winnipeg, MB R2C 5K6
Canada
204-866-3788
800-563-6127
Products: aromatherapy,
toiletries, bathing supply,
soap
Availability: boutiques,
specialty stores, mail order

Von Myering by Krystina
208 Seville Ave.
Pittsburgh, PA 15214
412-766-3186
Products: hair care, hair
color, permanents, nail care,
skin care for men and
women, sun care, bathing
supply
Availability: mail order

V'tae Parfum & Body Care
571 Searls Ave.
Nevada City, CA 95959
530-265-4255
800-643-3011
www.vtae.com
Products: aromatherapy,
fragrance for men and
women, skin care for men
and women
Availability: department
stores, health food stores,
cooperatives, V'tae Parfum
& Body Care stores,
boutiques, specialty stores,
mail order
MO

Wachters' Organic Sea Products
360 Shaw Rd.
S. San Francisco, CA 94080
650-588-9567
800-682-7100
www.wachters.com
Products: aromatherapy,
baby care, companion
animal care, hair care, hair
color, household supply,
laundry detergent, vitamins,
herbs
Availability: independent sales
representatives, mail order
MO

Wala-Heilmittel
P.O. Box 407
Wyoming, RI 02898
401-539-7037
800-499-7037
Products: skin care, toiletries
Availability: health food stores
V

Warm Earth Cosmetics
1155 Stanley Ave.
Chico, CA 95928-6944
530-895-0455
Products: cosmetics
Availability: department
stores, health food stores,
boutiques, specialty stores,
independent sales
representatives, mail order
MO

Weleda
175 North Route 9W
Congers, NY 10920
914-268-8572
800-241-1030
usa.weleda.com
Products: baby care, dental
hygiene, fragrance, hair
care, skin care, toiletries,
bathing supply, deodorant,
shaving supply, soap, herbs,
homeopathic medicines
Availability: drugstores,
health food stores,
cooperatives, Weleda store,
boutiques, specialty stores,
mail order
MO

The Wella Corporation
12 Mercedes Dr.
Montvale, NJ 07645
201-930-1020
800-526-4657
Products: hair care, hair
color, permanents
Availability: boutiques,
specialty stores, salons

Wellington Laboratories
1147 Stoneshead Ct., Suite B
Westlake Village, CA 91361
805-495-4824
800-835-8118
Products: baby care,
hypo-allergenic skin care,
toiletries, shaving supply
Availability: discount
department stores,
department stores,
drugstores, supermarkets,
cooperatives, boutiques,
specialty stores, distributors,
mail order

Dull looking skin?
Fix it in two minutes.

Nature's best exfoliants
reveal a soft, glowing complexion.

zia natural skincare

Whip-It Products
P.O. Box 30128
Pensacola, FL 32503
904-436-2125
800-582-0398
Products: household supply,
carpet cleaning supply,
laundry detergent, oven
cleaner, all-purpose cleaning
supply for home and
industrial use
Availability: independent
sales representatives, mail
order
V MO

Wind River Herbs
P.O. Box 3876
Jackson, WY 83001
307-733-6731
Products: herbal medicine
Availability: health food
stores, clinics, The Herb
Store, mail order
MO

WiseWays Herbals
Singing Brook Farm
99 Harvey Rd.
Worthington, MA 01098
413-238-4268
888-540-1600
www.wiseways.com
Products: aromatherapy,
baby care, feminine hygiene,
hair care, air freshener,
furniture polish, insect
repellant, skin care, bathing
supply, deodorant
Availability: department
stores, drugstores, health
food stores, cooperatives,
boutiques, specialty stores,
mail order
MO

Womankind
P.O. Box 1775
Sebastopol, CA 95473
707-522-8662
Products: feminine hygiene,
cloth menstrual pads
Availability: health food
stores, supermarkets,
cooperatives, boutiques,
specialty stores, independent
sales representatives, mail
order
MO

Wysong Corporation
1880 N. Eastman Rd.
Midland, MI 48642-7779
517-631-0009
800-748-0188
Products: companion animal
care, hair care, sun care,
toiletries, shaving supply,
vitamins
Availability: health food
stores, mail order
MO

Zia Natural Skincare
1337 Evans Ave.
San Francisco, CA 94124
415-642-8339
800-334-7546
www.zianatural.com
Products: aromatherapy,
cosmetics, skin care, sun
care
Availability: health food
stores, cooperatives,
boutiques, specialty stores,
mail order, Web site
MO

CATALOGS/STORES OFFERING CRUELTY-FREE PRODUCTS

The following catalog companies and stores
offer products not tested on animals.

Green Earth Office Supply
P.O. Box 719
Redwood Estates, CA
95044
800-327-8449
www.webcom.com/geos/
Products: office supply,
hemp, art supply
MO

The Heritage Store
P.O. Box 444
Virginia Beach, VA 23458
757-428-0100
800-862-2923
Products: aromatherapy,
dental hygiene, fragrance,
hair care, dandruff shampoo,
hypo-allergenic skin care,
sun care, toiletries, vitamins,
herbs, essential oil, health
care items
MO

**NOHARM (formerly WARM
Store)**
119 Turkey Hill Rd.
Northampton, MA 01062
413-587-0789
www.orbyss.com/noharm.htm
Products: buttons, stickers,
health and nutrition books,
T-shirts
V MO

Pangea Vegan Products
7829 Woodmont Ave.
Bethesda, MD 20814
301-652-3181
www.pangeaveg.com
Products: baby care,
companion animal care,
condoms, lubricants,
cosmetics, dental hygiene,
toothbrushes, feminine
hygiene, hair care,
household supply, laundry
detergent, nail care, razors,
skin care, sun care, toiletries
V MO

PETA
501 Front St.
Norfolk, VA 23510
757-622-7382
www.peta-online.org
Products: household supply,
laundry detergent, soap
V MO

Veg Essentials
7722 W. Menomonee River
Pkwy.
Wauwatosa, WI 53213
414-607-1953
877-881-6477
www.vegessentials.com
Products: aromatherapy,
baby care, companion
animal care, cosmetics,
dental hygiene, hair care, air
freshener, carpet cleaning
supply, laundry detergent,
insect repellant, skin care,
toiletries
V MO

QUICK REFERENCE GUIDE

Air Freshner

Amazon [V] 14
Ananda [V] 15
Aromaland 16
Aroma Vera 16
Auroma International [V] 17
Ayuerherbal 18
Basically Natural [V] 18
Bath & Body Works 18
Bath Island 18
Bella's Secret Garden 19
Crabtree & Evelyn 26
CYA Products [V] 27
Dr. Singha's [V] 29
Earth Friendly 29
Earthly Matters [V] 30
Ecco Bella 30
Essential Products [V] 32
Every Body 33
Liberty Natural [V] 47
Mother's [V] 51
Natura [V] 52
Natural Animal 52
Natural World 53
No Common Scents 56
Orange-Mate [V] 57
Oxyfresh [V] 58
Pathmark 58
PlantEssence 59
Pure & Basic [V] 60
Shadow Lake [V] 66
Sinclair & Valentine 66
Smith & Vandiver 67
Steps in Health 68
Terressentials [V] 70
Vermont Soapworks 73
WiseWays 76

Aromatherapy

ABEnterprises 12
Abra Therapeutics [V] 12
Ahimsa [V] 12
Alexandra Avery 12
Aloe Vera 14
American Safety 15

Apothecary Shoppe 15
Aromaland 16
Aroma Vera 16
Atmosa Brand [V] 16
Aura Cacia [V] 17
Australasian College 17
Autumn-Harp 17
Bare Escentuals 18
Basically Natural [V] 18
Bath & Body Works 18
Bath Island 18
Baudelaire 18
Beauty Without
    Cruelty [V] 19
Belle Star 19
Better Botanicals 19
Biotone 20
Body Encounters 20
Body Shop 20
Body Time 20
Börlind 21
Bronzo Sensualé [V] 22
Caswell-Massey 23
Celestial Body 23
Columbia Cosmetics 25
Common Scents 25
Compassion Matters 26
Countryside [V] 26
Derma-E 27
Desert Essence 28
Dr. Singha's [V] 29
Earth Science 30
Ecco Bella 30
Elizabeth Van Buren [V] 31
Essential Aromatics [V] 32
Essential Oil 32
Essential Products [V] 32
EuroZen [V] 33
Every Body 33
Face Food Shoppe 33
Faces by Gustavo 33
Faith Products 33
Forever Living 34
For Pet's Sake 34
Frontier Natural [V] 35
Herb Garden [V] 38
Home Health 38

InterNatural 39
Jacki's Magic 40
Jason Natural 40
Jeanne Rose 40
Katonah Scentral 42
KSA Jojoba [V] 44
La Crista [V] 44
Lady of the Lake [V] 45
Levlad 47
Liberty Natural [V] 47
Lotus Light 49
Mère Cie 50
Mia Rose [V] 50
Montagne Jeunesse 51
Natura [V] 52
Natural Bodycare [V] 53
Natural Science [V] 53
Natural World 53
Nature's Acres 53
Nirvana [V] 56
Rainforest 61
Royal Labs [V] 62
Santa Fe Botanical [V] 63
Sea-renity 65
Shadow Lake [V] 66
Shivani Ayurvedic 66
Simplers Botanical [V] 66
Sinclair & Valentine 66
Smith & Vandiver 67
Soap Opera [V] 67
Sumeru [V] 69
Sunfeather [V] 69
Sunshine Products [V] 70
Tisserand [V] 71
Vermont Soapworks 73
Virginia's Soap 74
V'tae Parfum 74
Wachters' 74
WiseWays 76
Zia 76

Baby Care

Ahimsa [V] 12
Arizona Natural 16
Aubrey Organics 16
Aura Cacia [V] 17

Autumn-Harp	17	Shadow Lake [V]	66	Amway	15
Basically Natural [V]	18	Shaklee	66	Astonish [V]	16
Bath & Body Works	18	Smith & Vandiver	67	Caeran	22
Bath Island	18	Studio Magic	68	Crown Royale [V]	27
Baudelaire	18	Sumeru [V]	69	Earthly Matters [V]	30
Bella's Secret	19	SunFeather [V]	69	Frank T. Ross [V]	34
Better Botanicals	19	Sunrise Lane	70	James Austin	40
Body Shop	20	Tom's of Maine	71	Lightning	47
Body Time	20	Vermont Soapworks	73	Natural World	53
Bronzo Sensualé	22	Wachters'	74	Nature Clean [V]	53
Caeran	22	Weleda	74	Pet Connection	59
Caswell-Massey	23	Wellington	74	Pets 'n People [V]	59
Compassion Matters	26	WiseWays	76	Rivers Run [V]	62
Country Comfort	26			Shadow Lake [V]	66
Crabtree & Evelyn	26	**Baking Soda**		Simple Wisdom	66
Dr. Bronner's [V]	28			Sunrise Lane	70
Earth Science	30	Food Lion	34	Vermont Soapworks	73
Earth Solutions [V]	30	Pathmark	58	Whip-It [V]	76
Essential Aromatics [V]	32				
Essential Oil	32	**Bleach**		**Companion Animal Care**	
Every Body	33				
Faces by Gustavo	33	Basically Natural [V]	18	Aloe Vera	14
Faith Products	33	Bio Pac [V]	20	Aubrey Organics	16
Food Lion	34	Country Save [V]	26	Ayurveda Holistic [V]	18
For Pet's Sake	34	Ecover	30	Basically Natural [V]	18
Healthy Times [V]	37	Frank T. Ross [V]	34	Brookside Soap [V]	22
Jacki's Magic	40	James Austin	40	Bug Off [V]	22
Jurlique	42	Kleen Brite	44	Caeran	22
Katonah Scentral	42	Nature Clean [V]	53	Carina	22
Kiehl's	44	Seventh Generation [V]	65	Crown Royale [V]	27
Kiss My Face	44	Sunrise Lane	70	Dallas Manufacturing	27
KSA Jojoba [V]	44			Dr. A.C. Daniels	28
La Crista	44	**Car Care**		Dr. Bronner's [V]	28
LaNatura [V]	45			Dr. Goodpet	29
Lander	45	Amway	15	Earth Solutions [V]	30
Liberty Natural [V]	47	Basically Natural [V]	18	Eco Design	30
Little Forest [V]	47	Caeran	22	Essential Aromatics [V]	32
Logona	48	For Pet's Sake	34	Forever Living	34
Lotus Light	49	Frank T. Ross [V]	34	Green Ban [V]	35
Magick Botanicals	49	IQ Products	39	Greentree	37
Mother's [V]	51	Natural World	53	Halo	37
Mountain Ocean	51	Nature Clean [V]	53	Herb Garden [V]	38
Naturade	52	Rivers Run [V]	62	Hewitt Soap	38
Natural Science [V]	53	Shadow Lake [V]	66	Home Health	38
Nature's Acres	53			IV Trail [V]	40
North Country	56	**Carpet Cleaning**		Jeanne Rose	40
Rainbow	61			K.B. Products	44
Reviva	61	Advanage [V]	12	Kenic Pet Products	44
Sacred Blends	62	Amazon [V]	14	KSA Jojoba [V]	44
Safeway	62	American		Lightning	47
Seventh Generation [V]	65	Formulating [V]	14	Lotus Light	49

Mallory 49
Mr. Christal's 52
Nala Barry [V] 52
Naturade 52
Natural Animal 52
Natural Chemistry 53
Naturally Yours [V] 53
Natural Products [V] 53
Natural Research [V] 53
Nature's Acres 53
Nature's Best [V] 55
Nature's Country [V] 55
Nature's Plus 55
No Common Scents 56
North Country 56
N/R Laboratories 56
Oxyfresh [V] 58
Pet Connection 59
PetGuard 59
Pets 'n People [V] 59
Professional Pet [V] 60
Pro-Tec 60
Real Animal Friends [V] 61
Rivers Run [V] 62
Simplers Botanical [V] 66
Sojourner Farms 68
Steps in Health 68
SunFeather [V] 69
Sunshine Natural [V] 70
Trophy 71
Veterinarian's Best [V] 73
Wachters' 74
Wysong 76

Condoms/Lubricants

Alexandra Avery 12
InterNatural 39
Lotus Light 49
Sagami [V] 63

Contact Lens Solution

Clear Conscience [V] 24
Lobob [V] 48

Cosmetics

Alexandra de Markoff 12
Almay 14
Aloette 14

Aloe Vera 14
Alvin Last 14
Amway 15
Arbonne 16
Arizona Natural 16
Aubrey Organics 16
Autumn-Harp 17
Aveda 17
Avon 17
Bare Escentuals 18
Basically Natural [V] 18
Bath & Body Works 18
BeautiControl 18
Beauty Without
    Cruelty [V] 19
Biogime [V] 20
Bio-Tec 20
Bobbi Brown 20
Bodyography 20
Body Shop 20
Bonne Bell 21
Börlind 21
Candy Kisses [V] 22
Chanel 23
Christian Dior 23
Christine Valmy 23
CiCi 23
Cinema Secrets [V] 23
Clarins of Paris 24
Clientele 25
Clinique 25
Color Me Beautiful 25
Color My Image 25
Columbia Cosmetics 25
Compassionate
    Consumer 25
Compassionate
    Cosmetics 25
Compassion Matters 26
Concept Now 26
Cosmair 26
Cosmyl 26
Decleor 27
Diamond Brands 28
Dr. Hauschka 29
Earth Science 30
E. Burnham 30
Ecco Bella 30
Elizabeth Grady 31
Estée Lauder 32
Eva Jon 33

Every Body 33
Faces by Gustavo 33
Fernand Aubry 33
Forever Living 34
For Pet's Sake 34
Garden Botanika 35
Georgette Klinger 35
Golden Pride 35
Hard Candy 37
Helen Lee 37
H2O Plus 38
Ida Grae 39
Il-Makiage 39
ILONA 39
i natural 39
InterNatural 39
Jane 40
Jennifer Tara 40
Joe Blasco 42
Jurlique 42
Kiehl's 44
Kiss My Face 44
KSA Jojoba [V] 44
La Costa 44
La Crista [V] 44
LaNatura [V] 45
Lancôme 45
La Prairie 45
L'Oréal 48
Lotus Light 49
M.A.C. 49
Magic of Aloe 49
Manic Panic 49
Marilyn Miglin 49
Mary Kay 49
Maybelline 50
Mehron 50
Merle Norman 50
Michael's Naturopathic 50
Mira Linder Spa 50
Narwhale 52
Naturade 52
Natural Science [V] 53
Nature's Plus 55
Neways [V] 55
Nutri-Metics 56
Ohio Hempery 57
Oriflame 57
Origins 58
Orjene 58
Orlane 58

Otto Basics	58
Parlux [V]	58
Patricia Allison	58
Paul Mazzotta [V]	59
Perfect Balance	59
Pierre Fabré	59
Prestige Cosmetics	60
Redken	61
Reviva	61
Revlon	61
Royal Labs [V]	62
Shaklee	66
Shivani Ayurvedic	66
Sombra	68
Spa Natural	68
Studio Magic	68
Sunrider	69
Tammy Taylor	70
TaUT	70
Terressentials [V]	70
Tish & Snooky's	70
Ultima II	71
Ultra Glow [V]	72
Urban Decay	72
Warm Earth	74
Zia	76

Dandruff Shampoo

ABBA [V]	12
Ahimsa [V]	12
Alvin Last	14
Amway	15
Avon	17
Bath Island	18
Beauty Naturally	18
Brocato [V]	22
Caeran	22
Carina	22
Citré Shine	24
Compassion Matters	26
Decleor	27
Derma E	27
Dermatologic Cosmetic	27
Earth Science	30
Ecco Bella	30
Every Body	33
For Pet's Sake	34
Home Health	38
InterNatural	39
Jason Natural	40

John Amico	42
J.R. Liggett [V]	42
Jurlique	42
K.B. Products	44
KMS Research	44
Lander	45
L'anza [V]	45
Logona	48
Mastey de Paris	50
Mill Creek	50
Murad	52
Naturade	52
Natural Bodycare [V]	53
Nature's Plus	55
Nexxus	55
Paul Mazzotta [V]	59
Pure & Basic [V]	60
Redken	61
Reviva	61
Sunshine Natural [V]	70
Thursday Plantation	70

Dental Hygiene

Aloe Vera	14
Alvin Last	14
Amway	15
Auroma International [V]	17
Auromère Ayurvedic [V]	17
Ayurherbal [V]	18
Basically Natural [V]	18
Bath Island	18
Beehive Botanicals	19
Body Shop	20
Caswell-Massey	23
Desert Essence	28
Eco-DenT	30
Eco Design	30
Forever Living	34
Katonah Scentral	42
Levlad	47
Liberty Natural [V]	47
Logona	48
Lotus Light	49
Natural World	53
Neways	55
NutriBiotic	56
Oxyfresh [V]	58
Pathmark	58
Shaklee	66
Steps in Health	68

Sunrider	69
Sunrise Lane	70
Thursday Plantation	70
Tom's of Maine	71
Weleda	75

Deodorant

ABEnterprises	12
Almay	14
Aloe Vera	14
Aramis	15
Aubrey Organics	16
Avalon [V]	17
Bare Escentuals	18
Bath & Body Works	18
Bath Island	18
Beauty Naturally	19
Body Shop	20
Caswell-Massey	23
Chanel	23
Clinique	25
Deodorant Stones [V]	27
Desert Essence	28
Dr. Hauschka	29
Earth Science	30
Estée Lauder	32
Every Body	33
Forever Living	34
For Pet's Sake	34
French Transit [V]	35
Garden Botanika	35
Hargen [V]	37
Jason Natural	40
Levlad	47
Liz Claiborne	48
Louise Bianco	49
Mill Creek	50
Nature de France [V]	53
North Country	56
Pure & Basic [V]	60
Queen Helene	61
Revlon	61
Shaklee	66
Shivani Ayurvedic	66
Soap Opera [V]	67
Steps in Health	68
Sunrise Lane	70
Terressentials [V]	70
Tom's of Maine	71
U.S. Sales [V]	72

Weleda	74
WiseWays	76

Ethnic Products

Almay	14
Aveda	17
Avon	17
Bobbi Brown	20
Citré Shine	24
Clinique	25
Jacki's Magic	40
John Amico	42
Kenra	44
Lander	45
M.A.C.	49
Maybelline	50
Origins	58
Prescriptives	60
Revlon	61

Feminine Hygiene

Celestial Body	23
Home Health	38
InterNatural	39
Jason Natural	40
Lotus Light	49
Natracare [V]	52
Seventh Generation [V]	65
WiseWays	76
Womankind	76

Fragrance for Men

Abercrombie & Fitch	12
Ahimsa [V]	12
Alexandra Avery	12
Aloette	14
Amway	15
Ananda [V]	15
Aramis	15
Aromaland	16
Aroma Vera	16
Aubrey Organics	16
Aura Cacia	17
Auroma International [V]	17
Avon	17
Ayurherbal [V]	18
Bare Escentuals	18
Baudelaire	18

BeautiControl	18
Belle Star	19
Better Botanicals	19
Body Shop	20
Caswell-Massey	23
Chanel	23
Christian Dior	23
Clientele	25
Common Scents	25
Compar	25
Cosmair	26
Crabtree & Evelyn	26
Crown Royale [V]	27
Decleor	27
Essential Oil	32
Fernand Aubry	33
Fragrance Impressions	34
Georgette Klinger	35
Hewitt Soap	38
Homebody	38
H2O Plus	38
ILONA	39
Katonah Scentral	42
Kiehl's	44
La Prairie	45
Logona	48
L'Orèal	48
Marilyn Miglin	49
Mêre Cie	50
Natura [V]	52
Natural Science [V]	53
Nature's Acres	53
Nectarine	55
No Common Scents	56
Oriflame	57
Parlux [V]	58
Perfect Balance	59
PlantEssence	59
Quan Yin [V]	60
Sante Fe Botanical [V]	63
Terressentials [V]	70
V'tae Parfum	74

Fragrance for Women

Ahimsa [V]	12
Alexandra Avery	12
Aloette	14
Amway	15
Ananda [V]	15
Aramis	15

Arbonne	16
Aromaland	16
Aroma Vera	16
Aubrey Organics	16
Aura Cacia [V]	17
Auroma International [V]	17
Avon	17
Ayurherbal [V]	18
Bare Escentuals	18
Bath & Body Works	18
Baudelaire	18
BeautiControl	18
Bella's Secret	19
Belle Star	19
Body Shop	20
Caswell-Massey	23
Chanel	23
Christian Dior	23
Clarins of Paris	24
Clientele	25
Clinique	25
Color Me Beautiful	25
Columbia Cosmetics	25
Common Scents	25
Compar	25
Compassion Matters	26
Cosmair	26
Cosmyl	26
Crabtree & Evelyn	26
Crown Royale [V]	27
Decleor	27
Donna Karan	28
Earth Science	30
Ecco Bella	30
Essential Aromatics [V]	32
Essential Oil	32
Essential Products [V]	32
Estée Lauder	32
Fernand Aubry	33
Forest Essentials	34
For Pet's Sake	34
Fragrance Impressions	34
Frontier Natural [V]	35
Garden Botanika	35
Georgette Klinger	35
Gryphon	37
Helen Lee	37
Henri Bendel	37
Herb Garden [V]	38
Hewitt Soap	38
Homebody	38

H2O Plus	38	**Furniture Polish**		Carina	22
ILONA	39			Carlson	22
Jason Natural	40	Amazon [V]	14	Caswell-Massey	23
Jessica McClintock	42	Amway	15	Chuckles	23
Katonah Scentral	42	Earth Friendly	29	Citré Shine	24
Kiehl's	44	Earthly Matters [V]	30	Clientele	25
KSA Jojoba [V]	44	Eco Design	30	Clinique	25
LaNatura [V]	45	Golden Pride	35	Columbia Cosmetics	25
La Prairie	45	InterNatural	39	Compassion Matters	26
Liberty Natural [V]	47	Natural World	53	Conair	26
Liz Claiborne	48	WiseWays	76	Decleor	27
L'Oréal	48			Derma-E	27
Lotus Light	49	**Hair Care**		Dermatologic Cosmetic	27
Marilyn Miglin	49			Desert Essence	28
Mary Kay	49	ABBA [V]	12	Dr. Bronner's [V]	28
Mère Cie	50	Abkit	12	Earth Friendly	29
Natura [V]	52	Ahimsa [V]	12	Earth Science	30
Natural Bodycare [V]	53	Aloe Up	14	E. Burnham	30
Natural Science [V]	53	Aloe Vera	14	Ecco Bella	30
Nature's Acres	53	Alvin Last	14	Edward & Sons	31
Nectarine	55	American		Espial [V]	31
No Common Scents	56	Formulating [V]	14	Essential Aromatics [V]	32
Nordstrom	56	Amitée	15	Every Body	33
Oriflame	57	Amway	15	Faith Products	33
Origins	58	Aramis	15	Focus 21	34
Orlane	58	Arbonne	16	Food Lion	34
Parlux [V]	58	Arizona Natural	16	Forever Living	34
Patricia Allison	58	Aroma Vera	16	For Pet's Sake	34
Perfect Balance	59	Aubrey Organics	16	Framesi	34
PlantEssence	59	Avalon [V]	17	Frank T. Ross [V]	34
Prescriptives	60	Aveda	17	Fruit of the Earth	35
Prestige Fragrances	60	Avon	17	Garden Botanika	35
Pure Touch [V]	60	Bare Escentuals	18	Georgette Klinger	35
Quan Yin [V]	60	Basically Natural [V]	18	Giovanni [V]	35
Ralph Lauren	61	Basic Elements [V]	18	Golden Pride	35
Redken	61	Bath & Body Works	18	Goldwell	35
Santa Fe Botanical [V]	63	Bath Island	18	Helen Lee	37
Shaklee	66	Beauty Naturally	19	Hobé	38
Shivani Ayurvedic	66	Beauty Without		Homebody	38
Simple Wisdom	66	Cruelty [V]	19	Home Health	38
Sinclair & Valentine	66	Beehive Botanicals	19	H2O Plus	38
Smith & Vandiver	67	Bella's Secret	19	Il-Makiage	39
Soap Opera [V]	67	Better Botanicals	19	i natural	39
Spa Natural	68	Bio-Tec	20	IQ Products	39
Sunrider	69	Body Shop	20	Jason Natural	40
Terra Nova	70	Body Time	20	Jheri Redding	42
Terressentials [V]	70	Börlind	21	John Amico	42
Tova	71	Botanics [V]	22	John Paul Mitchell [V]	42
Victoria's Secret	73	Brocato [V]	22	JOICO [V]	42
V'tae Parfum	74	Caeran	22	J.R. Liggett [V]	42
Weleda	74	CamoCare	22	Jurlique	42

Katonah Scentral	42	Reviva	61	Every Body	33
K.B. Products	44	Revlon	61	Farmavita	33
Ken Lange [V]	44	Royal Labs [V]	62	Framesi	34
Kenra	44	Rusk	62	Garnier	35
Kiehl's	44	Santa Fe Soap [V]	63	Goldwell	35
Kiss My Face	44	Scruples	65	Home Health	38
KMS Research	44	Sebastian	65	Il-Makiage	39
KSA Jojoba [V]	44	Shaklee	66	InterNatural	39
La Costa	44	Shikai	66	Jason Natural	40
Lander	45	Shivani Ayurvedic	66	John Amico	42
L'anza [V]	45	Simple Wisdom	66	JOICO [V]	42
Levlad	47	Soap Opera [V]	67	Katonah Scentral	42
Liberty Natural [V]	47	SoRik	68	L'anza [V]	45
Life Dynamics	47	Soya System	68	Logona	48
Logona	48	Spa Natural	68	L'Orèal	48
L'Orèal	48	Steps in Health	68	Manic Panic	49
Lotus Light	49	Stevens Research [V]	68	Mastey de Paris	50
M.A.C.	49	Sukesha	69	Nexxus	55
Magick Botanicals	49	Sunrider	69	Paul Mazzotta [V]	59
Magic of Aloe	49	Sunrise Lane	70	Rainbow	61
Mastey de Paris	50	Sunshine Natural [V]	70	Redken	61
Mill Creek	50	Supreme Beauty	70	Revlon	61
Mountain Ocean	51	Terressentials [V]	70	Scruples	65
Murad	52	Thursday Plantation	70	Sebastian	65
Natura [V]	52	Tisserand [V]	71	ShiKai	66
Naturade	52	Tom's of Maine	71	Soap Opera [V]	67
Natural Bodycare [V]	53	Tova	71	Sukesha	69
Natural World	53	Trader Joe's	71	Sunrise Lane	70
Nature Clean [V]	53	Travel Mates	71	Terressentials [V]	70
Nature de France [V]	53	Tressa	71	Tish & Snooky's	70
Nature's Plus	55	TRI Hair Care	71	Urban Decay	72
Nectarine	55	Von Myering [V]	74	Von Myering [V]	74
Neo Soma [V]	55	Wachters'	74	Wachters'	74
Neways	55	Weleda	74	Wella	74
Nexxus	55	Wella	74		
Nirvana [V]	56	WiseWays	76	**Household Supply**	
North Country	56	Wysong	76		
NuSkin	56			Advanage [V]	12
Oriflame	57	**Hair Color**		Allens Naturally [V]	14
Orjene	58			Aloe Vera	14
Oxyfresh [V]	58	Alvin Last	14	American	
Patricia Allison	58	Aubrey Organics	16	Formulating [V]	14
Paul Mazzotta [V]	59	Avigal Henna [V]	17	America's Finest [V]	15
Paul Mitchell [V]	59	Beauty Naturally	19	Amway	15
Perfect Balance	59	Bio-Tec	20	Ananda [V]	15
Pure & Basic [V]	60	Body Shop	20	Astonish [V]	16
Queen Helene	61	Carina	22	Aubrey Organics	16
Rainbow	61	Chuckles	23	Auroma International [V]	17
Rainforest	61	Conair	26	Ayurherbal [V]	18
Redken	61	Cosmair	26	Bath Island	18
Rejuvi	61	Earth Science	30	Bella's Secret	19

Bo-Chem	20	Seventh Generation [V]	65	Elizabeth Van Buren [V]	31
Bon Ami	21	Shadow Lake [V]	66	Essential Products [V]	32
Caeran	22	Shaklee	66	European Gold	32
Clear Vue [V]	24	Simple Wisdom	66	Face Food Shoppe	33
Compassionate		Sinclair & Valentine	66	Faces by Gustavo	33
Consumer	25	Stanhome	68	French Transit [V]	35
Compassion Matters	26	Steps in Health	68	Hawaiian Resources [V]	37
Cot 'n Wash [V]	26	Sunrider	69	Helen Lee	37
Country Save [V]	26	Terressentials [V]	70	Homebody	38
Crown Royale [V]	27	Trader Joe's	71	Ida Grae	39
DeSoto	28	Vapor Products	73	Il-Makiage	39
Earth Friendly	29	Vermont Soapworks	73	i natural	39
Earthly Matters [V]	30	Wachters'	74	Jason Natural	40
Ecco Bella	30	Whip-It [V]	76	Jeanne Rose	40
Ecover	30			La Crista [V]	44
Edward & Sons	31	**Hypo-Allergenic Skin Care**		Levlad	47
Espial [V]	31			Life Dynamics	47
Evans	33	Abra Therapeutics [V]	12	Logona	48
Faultless	33	Almay	14	L'Orèal	48
Food Lion	34	Aloe Up	14	Louise Bianco	49
Forever Living	34	Arbonne	16	M.A.C.	49
For Pet's Sake	34	Arizona Natural	16	Marché Image	49
Frank T. Ross [V]	34	Avalon [V]	17	Micro Balanced [V]	50
Frontier Natural [V]	35	Avon	17	Mira Linder Spa	50
Golden Pride	35	Bare Escentuals	18	Murad	52
H.e.r.c. [V]	38	Bath & Body Works	18	Narwhale	52
Home Health	38	BeautiControl	18	Naturade	52
Huish	39	Beauty Naturally	19	Natural Science [V]	53
Innovative [V]	39	Beauty Without		Natural World	53
James Austin	40	Cruelty [V]	19	Neocare [V]	55
J.C. Garet	40	Bella's Secret	19	Neways	55
Jurlique	42	Biogime [V]	20	North Country	56
Kleen Brite	44	Botan [V]	21	Oriflame	57
Liberty Natural [V]	47	Botanics [V]	22	Orlane	58
Life Tree [V]	47	Bronzo Sensualé [V]	22	Patricia Allison	58
Lightning	47	Caeran	22	Paul Mazzotta [V]	59
Lime-O-Sol	47	Carina	22	Perfect Balance	59
Mia Rose [V]	50	Celestial Body	23	Pharmagel [V]	59
Natural Animal	52	Christine Valmy	23	Pierre Fabré	59
Natural Bodycare [V]	53	Clarins of Paris	24	Pure & Basic [V]	60
Natural Chemistry	53	Clientele	25	Rainbow	61
Neocare [V]	55	Color My Image	25	Redken	61
New Age [V]	55	Crème de la Terre	27	Reviva Labs	61
Neway [V]	55	Decleor	27	Rivers Run [V]	62
Neways	55	Derma E	27	Royal Labs [V]	62
Nutri-Metics	56	Dermatologic Cosmetic	27	Shaklee	66
Oxyfresh [V]	58	Earth Science	30	Shirley Price	66
Planet [V]	59	E. Burnham	30	Sonoma Soap	68
Pure & Basic [V]	60	Ecco Bella	30	Spa Natural	68
Safeway	62	Eco Design	30	Studio Magic	68
SerVaas [V]	65	Elizabeth Grady	31	Sunrise Lane	70

Tammy Taylor	70	Ecover	30	Christian Dior	23
TaUT	70	Faith Products	33	Clarins of Paris	24
Thursday Plantation	70	Forever Living	34	Clinique	25
Tisserand [V]	71	Frank T. Ross [V]	34	Color My Image	25
Truly Moist	71	Golden Pride	35	Columbia Cosmetics	25
Tyra Skin Care	71	Home Service [V]	38	Cosmair	26
Vermont Soapworks	73	InterNatural	39	Cosmyl	26
Wellington	74	James Austin	40	Decleor	27
		Kleen Brite	44	Diamond Brands	28
Insect Repellant/Treatment		Life Tree [V]	47	Elizabeth Grady	31
		Natural World	53	Estée Lauder	32
Amway	15	Nature Clean [V]	53	Every Body	33
Aromaland	16	Oxyfresh [V]	58	Fernand Aubry	33
Aubrey Organics	16	Planet [V]	59	For Pet's Sake	34
Avon	17	Rivers Run [V]	62	Garden Botanika	35
Basically Natural [V]	18	Seventh Generation [V]	65	Georgette Klinger	35
Bath & Body Works	18	Shaklee	66	Hard Candy	37
Bug Off [V]	22	Simple Wisdom	66	Helen Lee	37
Compassion Matters	26	Sunrise Lane	70	Home Health	38
Essential Oil	32	Wachters'	74	H2O Plus	38
Fleabusters	33	Whip-It [V]	76	Il-Makiage	39
Green Ban [V]	35			InterNatural	39
Halo	37	**Laundry Detergent for Fine**		La Costa	44
Herb Garden [V]	38	**Washables**		Lee	47
Home Health	38			Liberty Natural [V]	47
InterNatural	39	Cot 'n Wash [V]	26	L'Orèal	48
IQ Products	39	Faith Products	33	M.A.C.	49
Jason Natural	40	Forever New [V]	34	Manic Panic	49
Liberty Natural [V]	47	Home Service [V]	38	Mary Kay	49
Lotus Light	49	Kleen Brite	44	Mira Linder Spa	50
Michael's Naturopathic	50			Nature's Plus	55
Natural Animal	52	**Makeup Brush (Vegan)**		Nectarine	55
North Country	56			Neways	55
SunFeather [V]	69	Origins	58	OPI Products	57
Terressentials [V]	70			Orlane	58
WiseWays	76	**Nail Care**		Orly	58
				Prestige	60
Laundry Detergent		Aloette	14	Revlon	61
		Amoresse	15	Smith & Vandiver	67
Advanage [V]	12	Andrea	15	Sunrider	69
Allens Naturally [V]	14	Ardell	16	Tammy Taylor	70
Aloe Vera	14	Avon	17	Tish & Snooky's	70
Amway	15	Bare Escentuals	18	Urban Decay	72
Basically Natural [V]	18	Bath & Body Works	18	Von Myering [V]	74
Bio Pac [V]	20	Bath Island	18		
Caeran	22	BeautiControl	18	**Office Supplies**	
Compassion Matters	26	Beauty Without			
Country Save [V]	26	Cruelty [V]	19	Berol	19
Earth Friendly	29	Body Shop	20	Citius [V]	23
Earthly Matters [V]	30	Bonne Bell	21	D.R.P.C. [V]	29
Eco Design	30	Chanel	23	Eberhard Faber	30

Evans	33
International Rotex [V]	39
Pilot [V]	59
Sanford	63
Staedtler	68

Paint

American Formulating [V]	14
Eco Design	30
Innovative [V]	39

Permanents

ABBA [V]	12
Beauty Naturally	19
Bio-Tec	20
Brocato [V]	22
Carina	22
Chuckles	23
Conair	26
Framesi	34
Jheri Redding	42
John Amico	42
JOICO [V]	42
Ken Lange [V]	44
KMS Research	44
L'anza [V]	45
L'Oréal	48
Mastey de Paris	50
Nexxus	55
Paul Mazzotta [V]	59
Redken	61
Scruples	65
Soya System	68
Stevens Research [V]	68
Sukesha	69
Sunrise Lane	70
Von Myering [V]	74
Wella	74

Razors

American Safety	15
Aramis	15
Bath Island	18
Body Shop	20
Compassion Matters	26
Crabtree & Evelyn	26
Norelco [V]	56

Pathmark	58
USA King's Crossing [V]	72

Shaving Supply

ABEnterprises	12
Abra Therapeutics [V]	12
Alba Botanica	12
Alexandra Avery	12
Aloe Vera	14
Alvin Last	14
American Safety	15
Aramis	15
Arbonne	16
Aubrey Organics	16
Bare Escentuals	18
Bath & Body Works	18
Bath Island	18
Body Shop	20
Body Time	20
Botan [V]	21
Caswell-Massey	23
Celestial Body	23
Christine Valmy	23
Clinique	25
Crabtree & Evelyn	26
Crown Royale [V]	27
Decleor	27
Earth Science	30
Ecco Bella	30
Eco Design	30
Estée Lauder	32
Every Body	33
Face Food Shoppe	33
Forever Living	34
Garden Botanika	35
Georgette Klinger	35
Golden Pride	35
Helen Lee	37
Homebody	38
H2O Plus	38
i natural	39
Jacki's Magic	40
Jason Natural	40
Katonah Scentral	42
Kiss My Face	44
La Costa	44
Lander	45
Levlad	47
Liz Claiborne	48
Logona	48

Magic of Aloe	49
Mill Creek	50
Natural	52
Nature's Acres	53
Nectarine	55
Neways	55
Origins	58
Orjene	58
Pure & Basic [V]	60
Redken	61
Reviva Labs	61
Royal Labs [V]	62
Shaklee	66
Shivani Ayurvedic	66
Sinclair & Valentine	66
Smith & Vandiver	67
Sunrider	69
Sunrise Lane	70
Surrey	70
Terressentials [V]	70
Tom's of Maine	71
USA King's Crossing [V]	72
Weleda	74
Wellington	74
Wysong	76

Skin Care

Abkit	12
Abra Therapeutics [V]	12
Alba Botanica	12
Alexandra Avery	12
Almay	14
Aloegen	14
Aloette	14
Aloe Up	14
Aloe Vera	14
Alvin Last	14
American International	14
Amway	15
Ancient Formulas	15
Andrea	15
Aramis	15
Arbonne	16
Ardell	16
Arizona Natural	16
Aroma Vera	16
Aubrey Organics	16
Aunt Bee's	16
Aura Cacia [V]	17
Auromère Ayurvedic [V]	17

Avalon [V]	17	Dermatologic Cosmetic	27	Kiehl's	44
Aveda	17	Desert Essence	28	Kiss My Face	44
Avon	17	Dr. Hauschka	29	KSA Jojoba [V]	44
Bare Escentuals	18	Earth Science	30	La Costa	44
Basically Natural [V]	18	Earth Solutions [V]	30	La Crista [V]	44
Basic Elements [V]	18	E. Burnham	30	LaNatura [V]	45
Bath & Body Works	18	Ecco Bella	30	La Prairie	45
Bath Island	18	Eco Design	30	Levlad	47
Baudelaire	18	Elizabeth Grady	31	Liberty Natural [V]	47
BeautiControl	18	Elizabeth Van Buren [V]	31	Life Dynamics	47
Beauty Naturally	19	Espial [V]	31	Lily of Colorado	47
Beauty Without		Essential Aromatics [V]	32	Logona	48
Cruelty [V]	19	Essential Products [V]	32	L'Oréal	48
Beehive Botanicals	19	Estée Lauder	32	Lotus Light	49
Beiersdorf	19	Eucerin	32	Louise Bianco	49
Bella's Secret	19	European Gold	32	M.A.C.	49
Better Botanicals	19	EuroZen [V]	33	Magick Botanicals	49
Biogime [V]	20	Evans	33	Magic of Aloe	49
Bio-Tec	20	Face Food Shoppe	33	Marché Image	49
Body Encounters	20	Faces by Gustavo	33	Marilyn Miglin	49
Body Shop	20	Facets	33	Mary Kay	49
Body Time	20	Faith Products	33	Mastey de Paris	50
Bonne Bell	21	Fernand Aubry	33	Merle Norman	50
Botan [V]	21	Forest Essentials	34	Michael's Naturopathic	50
Botanics [V]	22	Forever Living	34	Michelle Lazar	50
Bronzo Sensualé [V]	22	For Pet's Sake	34	Micro Balanced [V]	50
Caeran	22	Free Spirit [V]	35	Mill Creek	50
California SunCare	22	French Transit [V]	35	Mira Linder Spa	50
CamoCare	22	Fruit of the Earth	35	Montagne Jeunesse	51
Carina	22	Garden Botanika	35	Narwhale	52
Carlson	22	Georgette Klinger	35	Natura [V]	52
Caswell-Massey	23	Gigi Laboratories	35	Naturade	52
Celestial Body	23	Golden Pride	35	Natural Bodycare [V]	53
Chanel	23	Hawaiian Resources [V]	37	Natural Science [V]	53
Chatoyant Pearl	23	Helen Lee	37	Natural World	53
Christian Dior	23	Herb Garden [V]	38	Nature de France [V]	53
Christine Valmy	23	Hobé	38	Nature's Acres	53
Citré Shine	24	Homebody	38	Nature's Plus	55
Clarins of Paris	24	Home Health	38	Nectarine	55
Clientele	25	House of Cheriss	38	Neocare [V]	55
Clinique	25	H2O Plus	38	Neo Soma [V]	55
Color Me Beautiful	25	Ida Grae	39	Neways	55
Color My Image	25	Il-Makiage	39	New Chapter [V]	55
Columbia Cosmetics	25	ILONA	39	Nikken	55
Compassion Matters	26	i natural	39	Nirvana [V]	56
Concept Now	26	InterNatural	39	Nivea	56
Cosmyl	26	Jacki's Magic	40	Nordstrom	56
Crè me de la Terre	27	Jason Natural	40	North Country	56
Decleor	27	Jeanne Rose	40	NuSkin	56
Derma-E	27	Jennifer Tara	40	Nutri-Cell [V]	56
Dermalogica	27	John Paul Mitchell [V]	42	Ohio Hempery	57

Oriflame 57
Origins 58
Orjene 58
Orlane 58
Oxyfresh [V] 58
Patricia Allison 58
Paul Mazzotta [V] 59
Paul Mitchell [V] 59
Perfect Balance 59
Pharmagel [V] 59
Pierre Fabré 59
PlantEssence 59
Prescription Plus 60
Prescriptives 60
Principal Secret 60
Pure & Basic [V] 60
Quan Yin [V] 60
Queen Helene 61
Rachel Perry 61
Rainbow 61
Redken 61
Rejuvi 61
Reviva 61
Revlon 61
Rivers Run [V] 62
Royal Labs [V] 62
Sacred Blends 62
Sebastian 65
Shaklee 66
ShiKai 66
Shirley Price 66
Shivani Ayurvedic 66
Simple Wisdom 66
Sinclair & Valentine 66
Smith & Vandiver 67
Sombra 68
Sonoma Soap 68
Spa Natural 68
Steps in Health 68
Studio Magic 68
Sunrider 69
Sunrise Lane 70
Tammy Taylor 70
TaUT 70
Terressentials [V] 70
Thursday Plantation 70
Tisserand [V] 71
Tova 71
Truly Moist 71
Tyra Skin Care 71
Vermont Soapworks 73

Victoria's Secret 73
Von Myering [V] 74
V'tae Parfum 74
Wala-Heilmittel [V] 74
Weleda 74
Wellington 74
WiseWays 76
Zia 76

Sun Care/Tanning

Abra Therapeutics [V] 12
Alba Botanica 12
Alexandra Avery 12
Almay 14
Aloette 14
Aloe Up 14
Amway 15
Aramis 15
Arbonne 16
Arizona Natural 16
Aubrey Organics 16
Autumn-Harp 17
Avon 17
Basically Natural [V] 18
Bath & Body Works 18
Bath Island 18
BeautiControl 18
Beauty Without
   Cruelty [V] 19
Biogime [V] 20
Body Encounters 20
Body Shop 20
Body Time 20
Bonne Bell 21
Botanics [V] 22
Bronzo Sensualé [V] 22
Caeran 22
Chanel 23
Christine Valmy 23
Clarins of Paris 24
Clientele 25
Clinique 25
Color Me Beautiful 25
Color My Image 25
Columbia Cosmetics 25
Compassion Matters 26
Concept Now 26
Crème de la Terre 27
Decleor 27
Derma-E 27

Dermalogica 27
Dermatologic Cosmetic 27
Dr. Hauschka 29
Earth Science 30
Elizabeth Grady 31
Estée Lauder 32
European Gold 32
Every Body 33
Faces by Gustavo 33
Forest Essentials 34
Fruit of the Earth 35
Garden Botanika 35
Georgette Klinger 35
Golden Pride 35
Hawaiian Resources [V] 37
Helen Lee 37
H2O Plus 38
ILONA 39
i natural 39
InterNatural 39
Jason Natural 40
John Paul Mitchell [V] 42
Jurlique 42
Kiehl's 44
Kiss My Face 44
KSA Jojoba [V] 44
La Costa 44
Lancöme 45
La Prairie 45
Levlad 47
Logona 48
Louise Bianco 49
Magic of Aloe 49
Marché Image 49
Mary Kay 49
Mastey de Paris 50
Micro Balanced [V] 50
Mill Creek 50
Murad 52
Narwhale 52
Natural Bodycare [V] 53
Natural Science [V] 53
Natural World 53
Neways 55
North Country 56
NuSkin 56
Oriflame 57
Origins 58
Orjene 58
Orlane 58
Patricia Allison 58

Paul Mazzotta [V]	59	
Paul Mitchell [V]	59	
Perfect Balance	59	
Pierre Fabré	59	
Prescription Plus	60	
Prescriptives	60	
Rachel Perry	61	
Reviva	61	
Royal Labs [V]	62	
Shaklee	66	
SoRik	68	
Spa Natural	68	
Studio Magic	68	
Sunrider	69	
Tammy Taylor	70	
TaUT	70	
Thursday Plantation	70	
Tropix [V]	71	
Tyra Skin Care	71	
Ultra Glow [V]	72	
Victoria's Secret	73	
Von Myering [V]	74	
Wysong	76	
Zia	76	

Theatrical Makeup

Biogime [V]	20
Cinema Secrets [V]	23
Clientele	25
Color My Image	25
M.A.C.	49
Mehron	50
Sombra	68
Studio Magic	68
TaUT	70
Ultra Glow [V]	72
Urban Decay	72

Toiletries/Personal Care

Abercrombie & Fitch	12
Abra Therapeutics [V]	12
Alba Botanica	12
Alexandra Avery	12
Almay	14
Aloette	14
Aloe Up	14
Alvin Last	14
American International	14
American Safety	15
Amway	15
Aramis	15
Arizona Natural	16
Aroma Vera	16
Aunt Bee's	16
Aura Cacia [V]	17
Auroma International [V]	17
Auromère Ayurvedic [V]	17
Autumn-Harp	17
Avalon [V]	17
Aveda	17
Avon	17
Ayurherbal [V]	18
Bare Escentuals	18
Baudelaire	18
Beauty Without Cruelty [V]	19
Beehive Botanicals	19
Bella's Secret	19
Belle Star	19
Biokosma	20
Bio-Tec	20
Bobbi Brown	20
Body Encounters	20
Body Shop	20
Body Time	20
Bonne Bell	21
Bôrlind	21
Botan [V]	21
Caeran	22
Carlson	22
Carma	23
Caswell-Massey	23
Celestial Body	23
Chanel	23
Chatoyant Pearl	23
Christian Dior	23
Christine Valmy	23
Citré Shine	24
Clarins of Paris	24
Clearly Natural [V]	24
Clientele	25
Clinique	25
Color My Image	25
Compar	25
Compassionate Consumer	25
Compassionate Cosmetics	25
Conair	26
Cosmyl	26
Crabtree & Evelyn	26
Crème de la Terre	27
Crown Royale [V]	27
Decleor	27
Derma-E	27
Dermatologic Cosmetic	27
Desert Essence	28
Dr. Bronner's [V]	28
Dr. Hauschka	29
Earth Friendly	29
Earth Solutions [V]	30
Elizabeth Grady	31
English Ideas	31
Espial [V]	31
Essential Products [V]	32
Estée Lauder	32
Eva Jon	33
Every Body	33
Face Food Shoppe	33
Faces by Gustavo	33
Faith Products	33
Fernand Aubry	33
Forest Essentials	34
For Pet's Sake	34
French Transit [V]	35
Frontier Natural [V]	35
Garden Botanika	35
Georgette Klinger	35
Gryphon	37
Hawaiian Resources [V]	37
Helen Lee	37
Hewitt Soap	38
Homebody	38
Home Health	38
H2O Plus	38
i natural	39
InterNatural	39
Jacki's Magic	40
Jeanne Rose	40
Jheri Redding	42
Jurlique	42
Katonah Scentral	42
Kenra	44
Kiss My Face	44
KSA Jojoba [V]	44
La Costa	44
La Crista [V]	44
LaNatura [V]	45
Lander	45
Liberty Natural [V]	47
Life Dynamics	47

Life Tree [V]	47	Simple Wisdom	66	Auromêre Ayurvedic [V]	17
Liz Claiborne	48	Sinclair & Valentine	66	Australasian College	17
Logona	48	Smith & Vandiver	67	Ayurveda Holistic [V]	18
L'Orèal	48	Soap Opera [V]	67	Beehive Botanicals	19
Louise Bianco	49	Sonoma Soap	68	Caeran	22
M.A.C.	49	SoRik	68	Carlson	22
Magick Botanicals	49	Spa Natural	68	Clientele	25
Magic of Aloe	49	Steps in Health	68	Dr. Goodpet	29
Mastey de Paris	50	Sumeru [V]	69	Earth Science	30
Maybelline	50	SunFeather [V]	69	For Pet's Sake	34
Micro Balanced [V]	50	Sunrider	69	Freeda Vitamins	34
Mill Creek	50	Surrey	70	Frontier Natural [V]	35
Montagne Jeunesse	51	Tammy Taylor	70	Golden Pride	35
Mountian Ocean	51	TerraNova	70	Health Catalog	37
Naturade	52	Thursday Plantation	70	HealthRite	37
Natural	52	Tisserand [V]	71	Helen Lee	37
Natural Bodycare [V]	53	Tom's of Maine	71	Herbal Products	37
Natural World	53	Trader Joe's	71	Herb Garden [V]	38
Nature de France [V]	53	Travel Mates	71	Home Health	38
Nature's Acres	53	Upper Canada Soap	72	International Vitamin	39
Nature's Plus	55	Victoria's Secret	73	InterNatural	39
Nectarine	55	Virginia's Soap	74	Jeanne Rose	40
Neways	55	Wala-Heilmittel [V]	74	Liberty Natural [V]	47
Nexxus	55	Weleda	74	Lotus Light	49
NuSkin	56	Wellington	74	Magic of Aloe	49
NutriBiotic	56	Wysong	76	Michael's Naturopathic	50
Nutri-Metics	56			Montana Naturals	51
Oriflame	57	**Toothbrushes**		Natural World	53
Origins	58			Nature's Acres	53
Orjene	58	Bath Island	18	Nexxus	55
Oxyfresh [V]	58	Body Shop	20	Nutri-Cell [V]	56
Pacific Scents [V]	58	Caswell-Massey	23	Oriflame	57
Patricia Allison	58	Compassion Matters	26	Oxyfresh [V]	58
Paul Mazzotta [V]	59	Crabtree & Evelyn	26	Pathmark	58
PlantEssence	59	Eco-DenT	30	Sacred Blends	62
Prescriptives	60	Eco Design	30	Shaklee	66
Pure & Basic [V]	60	H2O Plus	38	Solgar	68
Quan Yin [V]	60	Katonah Scentral	42	Steps in Health	68
Queen Helene	61	Lotus Light	49	Studio Magic	68
Rainforest	61	Oxyfresh [V]	58	Sunrider	69
Redken	61	Pathmark	58	Terressentials [V]	70
Reviva	61	Safeway	62	Ultimate Life [V]	71
Revlon	61	Soap Opera [V]	67	Wachters'	74
Royal Labs [V]	62			Weleda	74
Safeway	62	**Vitamins/Herbs**		Wysong	76
Santa Fe Botanical [V]	63				
Shadow Lake [V]	66	ABEnterprises	12		
Shaklee	66	Abra Therapeutics [V]	12		
ShiKai	66	Aloe Vera	14		
Shivani Ayurvedic	66	Apothecary Shoppe	15		
Simplers Botanical [V]	66	Arbonne	16		

COMPANIES THAT TEST ON ANIMALS

Why Are These Companies Included on the "Do Test" List?

The following companies manufacture products that <u>ARE</u> tested on animals. Those marked with a check (✓) are presently observing a moratorium on animal testing. Please encourage them to announce a permanent ban. Listed in parentheses are either examples of products manufactured by that company or if applicable, its parent company. Companies on this list may manufacture individual lines of products without animal testing (e.g., Del Laboratories claims its Naturistics and Natural Glow lines are not animal-tested). They have not, however, eliminated animal testing on their entire line of cosmetics and household products.

Similarly, companies on this list may make some products, such as pharmaceuticals, that are required by law to be tested on animals. However, the reason for these companies' inclusion is not the <u>required</u> animal testing that they conduct, but rather the animal testing of personal care and household products that is <u>not</u> required by law.

What Can Be Done About Animal Tests Required by Law?

Although animal testing of certain pharmaceuticals and chemicals is still mandated by law, the same arguments against using animals in cosmetics testing are valid when applied to the pharmaceutical and chemical industries. These industries are regulated by the Food and Drug Administration and the Environmental Protection Agency, respectively, and animal tests for pharmaceuticals and chemicals are now required by law—laws that were developed haphazardly in the 1920s. We know that non-animal test methods exist <u>right now</u> and that these tests are more accurate in predicting toxicity than are crude, cruel tests on animals. It is the responsibility of the companies that kill animals in order to bring their products to market to convince the regulatory agencies that there is a better way to determine product safety. Companies resist progress because the crude nature of animal tests allows them to market many products that might be determined too toxic if cell culture tests were used. Let companies know how you feel about this.

Alberto-Culver (Tresemmé,
Sally Beauty Supply, Alberto
V05, TCB Naturals)
2525 W. Armitage Ave.
Melrose Park, IL 60160
708-450-3000
www.alberto.com

Allergan, Inc.
2525 Dupont Dr.
P.O. Box 19534
Irvine, CA 92612
714-752-4500
800-347-4500
corpinfo@allergan.com

Arm & Hammer (Church &
Dwight)
P.O. Box 1625
Horsham, PA 19044-6625
609-683-5900
800-524-1328
www.armhammer.com

Bausch & Lomb (Clear
Choice)
1 Bausch & Lomb Place
Rochester, NY 14604-2701
716-338-6000
800-344-8815
www.bausch.com

Benckiser (Coty, Lancaster,
Jovan)
237 Park Ave., 19th Fl.
New York, NY 10017-3142
212-850-2300
attmail@cotyusa.com

✓ Bic Corporation
500 Bic Dr.
Milford, CT 06460
203-783-2000

Block Drug Co., Inc.
(Polident, Sensodyne,
Tegrin, Lava, Carpet Fresh)
257 Cornelison Ave.
Jersey City, NJ 07302
201-434-3000
800-365-6500

Boyle-Midway (Reckitt &
Colman)
2 Wickman Rd.
Toronto, ON M8Z 5M5
Canada
416-255-2300

✓ Braun (Gillette
Company)
400 Unicorn Park Dr.
Woburn, MA 01801
800-272-8611
braun_usa@braun.de

Bristol-Myers Squibb Co.
(Clairol, Ban Roll-On, Keri,
Final Net)
345 Park Ave.
New York, NY 10154-0037
212-546-4000
www.bms.com

Calvin Klein (Unilever)
725 Fifth Ave.
New York, NY 10022-2519
212-759-8888
800-745-9696
www.unilever.com

Carter-Wallace (Arrid,
Lady's Choice, Nair, Pearl
Drops)
1345 Ave. of the Americas
New York, NY 10105-0021
212-339-5000

Chesebrough-Ponds
(Fabergé, Cutex, Vaseline)
800 Sylvan Ave.
Englewood Cliffs, NJ 07632
800-243-5804

Church & Dwight (Arm &
Hammer)
P.O. Box 1625
Horsham, PA 19044-6625
609-683-5900
800-524-1328
www.armhammer.com

Clairol, Inc. (Bristol-Myers
Squibb)
40 W. 57th St., 23rd fl.
New York, NY 10019
212-541-2740
800-223-5800
www.bms.com

Clorox (Pine-Sol, S.O.S.,
Tilex, ArmorAll)
1221 Broadway
Oakland, CA 94612
510-271-7000
800-227-1860
www.clorox.com

Colgate-Palmolive Co.
(Palmolive, Ajax, Fab, Speed
Stick, Mennen, SoftSoap)
300 Park Ave.
New York, NY 10022
212-310-2000
800-221-4607
www.colgate.com

Coty (Benckiser)
237 Park Ave., 19th Fl.
New York, NY 10017-3142
212-850-2300
www.cotyusainc.com

Cover Girl (Procter &
Gamble)
One Procter & Gamble
Plaza
Cincinnati, OH 45202
513-983-1100
800-543-1745
www.covergirl.com

Dana Perfumes (Alyssa
Ashley)
470 Oak Hill Rd.
Mountain Top, PA 18707
800-822-8547
www.beautyspot.com

Del Laboratories (Flame
Glow, Commerce Drug,
Sally Hansen)
565 Broad Hollow Rd.
Farmingdale, NY 11735
516-293-7070
800-645-9888
www.dellabs.com

✓ Dial Corporation (Purex,
Renuzit)
15101 N. Scottsdale Rd.
Suite 5028
Scottsdale, AZ 85254-2199
602-207-1800
800-528-0849
www.dialcorp.com

DowBrands (Glass Plus,
Fantastik, Vivid)
P.O. Box 68511
Indianapolis, IN 46268
317-873-7000
www.dowclean.com

Drackett Products Co. (S.C.
Johnson & Son)
1525 Howe St.
Racine, WI 53403
414-631-2000
800-558-5252
www.scjohnsonwax.com

Elizabeth Arden (Unilever)
390 Park Ave.
New York, NY 10022
212-888-1260
800-745-9696
www.unilever.com

Erno Laszlo
89 Park View Ave.
W. Harrison, NY 10604
800-511-7364

✓ Gillette Co. (Liquid
Paper, Flair, Braun,
Duracell)
Prudential Tower Bldg.
Boston, MA 02199
617-421-7000
800-872-7202
www.gillette.com

Givaudan-Roure
1775 Windsor Rd.
Teaneck, NJ 07666
201-833-2300

Helene Curtis Industries
(Finesse, Unilever, Suave)
800 Sylvan Ave.
Englewood Cliffs, NJ 07632
800-621-2013
www.unilever.com

Jhirmack (Playtex)
300 Nyala Farms Rd.
Westport, CT 06880
203-341-4000

Johnson & Johnson
(Neutrogena)
1 Johnson & Johnson Plaza
New Brunswick, NJ 08933
908-524-0400
www.jnj.com

Kimberly-Clark Corp.
(Kleenex, Scott Paper,
Huggies)
P.O. Box 619100
Dallas, TX 75261-9100
800-544-1847
www.kimberly-clark.com

Lamaur
5601 E. River Rd.
Fridley, MN 55432
612-571-1234

Lever Bros. (Unilever)
800 Sylvan Ave.
Englewood Cliffs, NJ 07632
212-888-1260
800-598-1223
www.unilever.com

Max Factor (Procter &
Gamble)
One Procter & Gamble
Plaza
Cincinnati, OH 45202
513-983-1100
800-543-1745
www.maxfactor.com

Mead
Courthouse Plaza N.E.
Dayton, OH 45463
937-495-3312
www.mead.com

Melaleuca, Inc.
3910 S. Yellowstone Hwy.
Idaho Falls, ID 83402-6003
208-522-0700

Mennen Co. (Colgate-
Palmolive)
E. Hanover Ave.
Morristown, NJ 07962
201-631-9000
www.colgate.com

Neoteric Cosmetics
4880 Havana St.
Denver, CO 80239-0019
303-373-4860

Noxell (Procter & Gamble)
11050 York Rd.
Hunt Valley, MD 21030-
2098
410-785-7300
800-572-3232
www.pg.com

Olay Co./Oil of Olay
(Procter & Gamble)
P.O. Box 599
Cincinnati, OH 45201
800-543-1745
www.oilofolay.com

✓ Oral-B (Gillette
Company)
1 Lagoon Dr.
Redwood City, CA 94065-
1561
415-598-5000
www.oralb.com

Pantene (Procter & Gamble)
Procter & Gamble Plaza
Cincinnati, OH 45202
800-945-7768
www.pg.com

Parfums International
(White Shoulders)
1345 Ave. of the Americas
New York, NY 10105
212-261-1000

✓ Parker Pens (Gillette
Company)
P.O. Box 5100
Janesville, WI 53547-5100
608-755-7000
braun_usa@braun.de

Perrigo
117 Water St.
Allegan, MI 49010
616-673-8451
800-253-3606
www.perrigo.com

95

Pfizer, Inc. (Bain de Soleil, Plax, Visine, Desitin, BenGay, Barbasol)
235 E. 42nd St.
New York, NY 10017-5755
212-573-2323
www.pfizer.com

Playtex Products, Inc. (Banana Boat, Woolite, Jhirmack)
300 Nyala Farms Rd.
Westport, CT 06880
203-341-4000
www.playtex.com

Procter & Gamble Co. (Crest, Tide, Cover Girl, Max Factor, Giorgio)
One Procter & Gamble Plaza
Cincinnati, OH 45202
513-983-1100
800-543-1745
www.pg.com/info

Reckitt & Colman (Lysol, Mop & Glo)
1655 Valley Rd.
Wayne, NJ 07474-0945
201-633-6700
800-232-9665

Richardson-Vicks (Procter & Gamble)
One Procter & Gamble Plaza
Cincinnati, OH 45202
513-983-1100
800-543-1745
www.pg.com/info

Sally Hansen (Del Laboratories)
565 Broad Hollow Rd.
Farmingdale, NY 11735
516-293-7070
800-645-9888
www.sallyhansen.com

Sanofi (Oscar de la Renta, Yves Saint Laurent)
90 Park Ave., 24th Fl.
New York, NY 10016
212-551-4757

Schering-Plough (Coppertone)
1 Giralda Farms
Madison, NJ 07940-1000
201-822-7000
800-842-4090
www.sch-plough.com

Schick (Warner-Lambert)
201 Tabor Rd.
Morris Plains, NJ 07950
201-540-2000
800-492-1555
www.warner-lambert.com

S.C. Johnson & Son (Pledge, Drano, Windex, Glade)
1525 Howe St.
Racine, WI 53403
414-260-2000
800-558-5252
www.scjohnsonwax.com

SmithKline Beecham
100 Beecham Dr.
Pittsburgh, PA 15205
412-928-1000
800-456-6670
www.sb.com

SoftSoap Enterprises (Colgate-Palmolive)
300 Park Ave.
New York, NY 10022
800-221-4607
www.colgate.com

Sun Star
600 Eagle Dr.
Bensenville, IL 60106-1977
800-821-5455

3M (Scotch, Post-It)
Center Bldg., 220-2E-02
St. Paul, MN 55144-1000
612-733-1110
800-364-3577
www.3m.com

Unilever (Lever Bros., Calvin Klein, Elizabeth Arden, Helene Curtis, Diversey)
800 Sylvan Ave.
Englewood Cliffs, NJ 07632
212-888-1260
800-598-1223
www.unilever.com

Vidal Sassoon (Procter & Gamble)
P.O. Box 599
Cincinnati, OH 45202
800-543-7270
www.pg.com

Warner-Lambert (Lubriderm, Listerine, Schick)
201 Tabor Rd.
Morris Plains, NJ 07950-2693
201-540-2000
800-323-5379
www.warner-lambert.com

PEOPLE WHO ARE
VIOLENT
TO ANIMALS
RARELY STOP THERE

Studies show that people who abuse their companion animals are likely to abuse their kids. So if you see an animal mistreated or neglected, please report it. Because the parent who comes home and kicks the dog is probably just warming up.

Call for Information • 757-622-PETA

PeTA PEOPLE FOR THE ETHICAL TREATMENT OF ANIMALS
501 FRONT ST., NORFOLK, VA 23510 • www.peta-online.org

A Shopper's Guide to Leather Alternatives

Having trouble finding non-leather dress shoes or hiking boots for your entire family? Looking for wallets, bags, belts, briefcases, and other items made without the use of animals?

This 8-page guide offers a list of mail-order companies selling everything from non-leather baseball gloves, ice skates, rock climbing shoes, and tool belts to vegan biking gloves, Western-style boots, work boots, and much more. You'll also find suggestions about which stores tend to carry a wide selection of non-leather items.

This guide is certain to make your shopping days easier! To order, send $4 to the address below.

Other valuable guides available from VRG include:

The Vegan Diet During Pregnancy, Lactation, and Childhood $3
Guide to Food Ingredients $4
Vegetarian and Vegan Menu Items at Fast Food
and Quick Service Restaurant Chains $4

To order any of these items, please send a check or money order to The Vegetarian Resource Group, PO Box 1463, Baltimore, MD 21203 or call (410) 366-8343 weekdays between 9am and 6pm EST to charge your order with a Visa or Mastercard. You can also fax your order to (410) 366-8804 or place your order at our website:
www.vrg.org

Alternatives to Leather
and
Other Animal Products

Many animals from whom skins and other body parts are obtained suffer all the horrors of factory farming, including extreme crowding and confinement, deprivation, unanesthetized castration, branding, tail-docking, and de-horning, and cruel treatment during transport and slaughter. As a result, more and more people are realizing that animal products are something we can do without.

Alternatives to leather can be found just about anywhere you might shop. But some places, such as discount shoe and variety stores, like Payless Shoe Source, Fayva, Kmart, J.C. Penney, Marshall's, and Wal-Mart, offer larger selections. Designers like Liz Claiborne, Capezio, Sam & Libby, Unlisted by Kenneth Cole, and Nike (call 1-800-344-NIKE for a current list of vegan styles) offer an array of nonleather handbags, wallets, and shoes.

For more shopping tips, send for *The Compassionate Shopper* (Beauty Without Cruelty, 175 W. 12th St., #16G, New York, NY 10011-8275) or "A Shopper's Guide to Leather Alternatives" (The Vegetarian Resource Group, P.O. Box 1463, Baltimore, MD 21203).

The following is a list of mail-order companies that specialize in nonleather clothing and accessories:

Aesop, Inc.
P.O. Box 315
N. Cambridge, MA 02140
617-628-8030

ExTredz
388 Carlaw Ave.
Unit 100D
Toronto, ON
M4M 2T4 Canada
416-406-1876
www.extredz.com

Heartland Products
Box 218
Dakota City, IA 50529
800-441-4692

Ohio Hempery
7002 State Rte. 329
Guysville, OH 45735
800-BUY-HEMP

Pangea
7829 Woodmont Ave.
Bethesda, MD 20814
301-652-3181

Used Rubber USA
597 Haight St.
San Francisco, CA 94117
415-626-7855

Vegetarian Shoes
12 Gardner St.
Brighton BN1 1UP
England
011-441-273-691913

WHAT WOULD YOU DO TO SAVE AN ANIMAL?

Animals have long held a special place in my heart—their companionship has always been very important to me. That's why it distresses me to tell you that tens of thousands of animals are suffering needlessly.

They desperately need help—and organizations like PETA.

Since 1980, People for the Ethical Treatment of Animals has become this nation's most effective advocate in behalf of animal protection. The people at PETA are committed to exposing and stopping animal cruelty—especially in laboratories.

It feels great to use my voice for animals. Please join me and contact PETA today. *You* can help save animals, too.

For more information on how you can become part of this vital work, write: PETA, 501 Front St., Norfolk, VA 23510, or call 757-622-PETA.

Rue

100

HEALTH CHARITIES: HELPING OR HURTING?

When you donate to a charity, do you know where the money actually goes? Could your gift be contributing to animal suffering?

Some health charities ask for donations to help people with diseases and disabilities yet spend the money to bankroll horrific experiments on dogs, rabbits, rats, mice, primates, hamsters, pigs, ferrets, frogs, fish, guinea pigs, sheep, birds, and other animals. While human health needs cry out for attention and so many people are going without medical care, animal experimentation enriches laboratories and scientists but drains money from relevant and effective projects that could really help save lives.

Healing Without Hurting

Instead of pillaging animals' bodies for cures for human diseases, compassionate charities focus their research where the best hope of treatment lies: with humans.

They realize that animal experiments are unnecessary, unreliable, and sometimes dangerously misleading. Enormous variations exist among rats, rabbits, dogs, pigs, and human beings, and meaningful scientific conclusions cannot be drawn about one species by studying another. Non-animal methods provide a more accurate method of testing and can be interpreted more objectively.

Compassionate, modern charities know that we can improve treatments through up-to-date, non-animal methods, and they fund only non-animal research, leading to real progress in the prevention and treatment of disease—without starving, crippling, burning, poisoning, or cutting open animals.

HEALTH CHARITIES THAT DON'T TEST ON ANIMALS

What Types of Charities Are on the "Don't Test" List?

Health charities and service organizations that do not conduct or fund experiments on animals are included on the "don't test" list. These organizations deal with human health issues ranging from birth defects to heart disease to substance abuse. Some fund non-animal research to find treatments and cures for diseases and disabilities while others provide services and direct care to people living with physical or mental ailments.

How Does a Charity Get on the List?

Charities that are listed have signed PETA's statement of assurance certifying that neither they nor their affiliated organizations conduct or fund any experiments on animals and will not do so in the future. Those marked with an asterisk (*) are presently observing a moratorium on (i.e., current suspension of) animal experiments.

Please contact PETA if you know the address of a charity that is not listed, including local health service organizations. PETA will be happy to inquire about a charity's animal-testing policy, but we also encourage you to inquire, as it is important that charities hear directly from compassionate citizens who are opposed to animal testing.

*   *   *

The following health charities and service organizations DO NOT conduct or fund animal experiments. They may deal with several issues, including nonhealth-related issues, but they are listed according to their primary health focus. For more information on the programs and activities of an organization, please contact the organization.

AIDS/HIV

Charlotte HIV/AIDS
Network, Inc. (CHAN)
P.O. Box 4229
Port Charlotte, FL 33949-4229
941-625-6650
941-625-AIDS

Chicago House
1925 N. Clayburn, Suite 401
Chicago, IL 60614
312-248-5200

Children's Immune Disorder
16888 Greenfield Rd.
Detroit, MI 48235-3707
313-837-7800

Concerned Citizens for
Humanity
3580 Main St., Suite 115
Hartford, CT 06120-1121
860-560-0833

Design Industries
Foundation Fighting AIDS
(DIFFA)
150 W. 26th St., Suite 602
New York, NY 10001
212-645-0534

Health Cares Exchange
Initiative, Inc.
P.O. Box 31
The State House
Boston, MA 02133
617-499-7780

Joshua Tree Feeding
Program, Inc.
P.O. Box 7056
Phoenix, AZ 85011-7056
602-264-0223

Loving Arms
P.O. Box 3368
Memphis, TN 38173
901-725-6730

Miracle House
P.O. Box 30931
New York, NY 10011-0109
212-367-9281

Phoenix Shanti Group, Inc.
2020 W. Indian School Rd.
#50
Phoenix, AZ 85015
602-279-0008

Puerto Rico Community
Network for Clinical
Research on AIDS
One Stop Station, #30
P.O. Box 70292
San Juan, PR 00936-8292
809-753-9443

Santa Fe Cares
P.O. Box 1255
Santa Fe, NM 87504-1255
505-989-9255
www.santafecares.org

ARTHRITIS

Arthritis Fund aka The
Rheumatoid Disease
Foundation
5106 Old Harding Rd.
Franklin, TN 37064
615-646-1030
taf@telalink.net

BIRTH DEFECTS

Association of Birth Defect
Children, Inc.
827 Irma Ave.
Orlando, FL 32803
800-313-2232
www.birthdefects.org

Little People's Research
Fund, Inc.
80 Sister Pierre Dr.
Towson, MD 21204
800-232-5773

National Craniofacial
Association
P.O. Box 11082
Chattanooga, TN 37401
800-332-2373

Puerto Rico Down
Syndrome Foundation
P.O. Box 195273
San Juan, PR 00919-5273
787-268-DOWN

Warner House
1023 E. Chapman Ave.
Fullerton, CA 92831
714-441-2600

BLIND, VISUALLY
IMPAIRED

American Association of the
Deaf-Blind
814 Thayer Ave., Suite 302
Silver Spring, MD 20910-
4500

Collier County Association
for the Blind
4701 Golden Gate Pkwy.
Naples, FL 34116
941-649-1122

Connecticut Institute for the
Blind/Oak Hill
120 Holcomb St.
Hartford, CT 06112-1589
860-242-2274

Cumberland County
Association for the Blind
837 Robeson St.
Fayetteville, NC 28305
910-483-2719

Deaf-Blind Service Center
2366 Eastlake Ave. E.
Suite 206
Seattle, WA 98102
206-323-9178

Independence for the Blind,
Inc.
1278 Paul Russell Rd.
Tallahassee, FL 32301
904-942-3658

Living Skills Center for
Visually Impaired
13830-B San Pablo Ave.
San Pablo, CA 94806
510-234-4984

National Federation of the
Blind, Inc.
1800 Johnson St
Baltimore, MD 21230
410-659-9314

Radio Information Service
2100 Wharton St.
Suite 140
Pittsburgh, PA 15203
412-488-3944

VISIONS/Services for the
Blind and Visually Impaired
500 Greenwich St., 3rd Fl
New York, NY 10013-1354
888-245-8333
www.visionsvcb.org

Washington Volunteer
Readers for the Blind
901 G St. N.W.
Washington, DC 20001
202-727-2142

BLOOD

Michigan Community Blood
Centers
P.O. 1704
Grand Rapids, MI 49501-1704
800-742-6317

BURNS

Children's Burn Foundation
4929 Van Nuys Blvd.
Sherman Oaks, CA 91403
818-907-2822

CANCER

Calvary Fund, Inc.
Calvary Hospital
1740 Eastchester Rd.
Bronx, NY 10461

Cancer Care Services
605 W. Magnolia
Ft. Worth, TX 76104
817-921-0653

Cancer Prevention and
Survival Fund, c/o PCRM
5100 Wisconsin Ave. N.W.
Suite 404
Washington, DC 20016
202-686-2210

Danville Cancer
Association, Inc.
1225 W. Main St.
P.O. Box 2148
Danville, VA 24541
804-792-3700

Miracle House
P.O. Box 30931
New York, NY 10011-0109
212-367-9281

National Children's Cancer
Society
1015 Locust, Suite 1040
St. Louis, MO 63101
314-241-1600

Quest Cancer Research
Woodbury, Harlow Rd.
Roydon, Harlow, Essex
CM19 5HF
01279 792233

Skin Cancer Foundation
245 Fifth Ave., Suite 1403
New York, NY 10016
800-754-6490

Tomorrows Children's Fund
Hackensack University
Medical Center
30 Prospect Ave.
Hackensack, NJ 07601
201-996-5500

CHILDREN

Association of Birth Defect
Children, Inc.
827 Irma Ave.
Orlando, FL 32803
800-313-2232
www.birthdefects.org

Children's Burn Foundation
4929 Van Nuys Blvd.
Sherman Oaks, CA 91403
818-907-2822

Children's Diagnostic
Center, Inc.
2100 Pleasant Ave.
Hamilton, OH 45015

Children's Immune Disorder
16888 Greenfield Rd.
Detroit, MI 48235-3707
313-837-7800

Children's Wish Foundation
International
8615 Roswell Rd.
Atlanta, GA 30350-4867
800-323-WISH

Crestwood Children's
Center
2075 Scottsville Rd.
Rochester, NY 14623-2098
716-436-4442

Eagle Valley Children's Home
2300 Eagle Valley Ranch Rd.
Carson City, NV 89703
702-882-1188

Five Acres/The Boys' and
Girls' Aid Society of Los
Angeles
760 W. Mountain View St.
Altadena, CA 91001
818-798-6793
213-681-4827
www.5acres.org

Help Hospitalized
Children's Fund
10723 Preston Rd., #132
Dallas, TX 75230-3806
214-696-4843

Miracle Flights
2756 N. Green Valley Pkwy.
Suite 115
Green Valley, NV 89014-2100
800-FLY-1711

National Children's Cancer
Society
1015 Locust, Suite 1040
St. Louis, MO 63101
314-241-1600

Pathfinder International
9 Galen St., Suite 217
Watertown, MA 02172-4501
617-924-7200

Rainbow Kids
P.O. Box 70844
Richmond, VA 23255
804-288-0479

Tomorrows Children's Fund
Hackensack University
Medical Center
30 Prospect Ave.
Hackensack, NJ 07601
201-996-5500

DEAF/HEARING-IMPAIRED

Be an Angel Fund
T.H. Rogers School
5840 San Felipe
Houston, TX 77057
713-917-3568

Better Hearing Institute
P.O. Box 1840
Washington, DC 20013
800-EAR-WELL
www.betterhearing.org

Chicago Hearing Society
332 S. Michigan Ave.
Suite 714
Chicago, IL 60604
312-939-6888
dhhs@lancnews.infi.net

Deaf Action Center
3115 Crestview Dr.
Dallas, TX 75235
214-521-0407

Deaf-Blind Service Center
2366 Eastlake Ave. E.
Suite 206
Seattle, WA 98102
206-323-9178

Deaf Independent Living
Association, Inc.
P.O. Box 4038
Salisbury, MD 21803-4038
410-742-5052

Deaf Service Center of St.
Johns County
207 San Marco Ave., #38
St. Augustine, FL 32084-2762

Institute for Rehabilitation,
Research, and Recreation,
Inc.
P.O. Box 1025
Pendleton, OR 97801
541-276-2752

League for the Hard of
Hearing
71 W. 23rd St.
New York, NY 10010-4162
212-741-7650
www.lhh.org

Minnesota State Academy
for the Deaf
P.O. Box 308
Faribault, MN 55021
800-657-3996

DISABLED,
DEVELOPMENTALLY

Achievements, Inc.
101 Mineral Ave.
Libby, MT 59923
406-293-8848

Adult Training and
Habilitation Center
311 Fairlawn Ave. W.
Box 600
Winsted, MN 55395
612-485-4191

Association for Community
Living
One Carando Dr.
Springfield, MA 01104-3211
413-732-0531

Burnt Mountain Center
P.O. Box 337
Jasper, GA 30143
706-692-6016

Butler Valley, Inc.
380 12th St.
Arcata, CA 95521

Career Development Center
2110 W. Delaware
Fairfield, IL 62837

Carroll Haven Achieving
New Growth Experiences
(CHANGE)
115 Stoner Ave.
Westminster, MD 21157-5443
410-876-2179

Community Services
452 Delaware Ave.
Buffalo, NY 14202-1515
716-883-8888

Concerned Citizens for the
Developmentally Disabled
P.O. Box 725
303B S. Washington St.
Chillicothe, MO 64601
816-646-0109

Creative Employment
Opportunities
50711 Wing Dr.
Shelby Twp., MI 48315
810-566-4770

DeWitt County Human
Resource Center
1150 Route 54 W.
Clinton, IL 61727
217-935-9496

Eagle Valley Children's
Home
2300 Eagle Valley Ranch Rd.
Carson City, NV 89703
702-882-1188

EYAS Corporation
411 Scarlet Sage St.
Punta Gorda, FL 33950
813-575-2255

Hartville Meadows
P.O. Box 1055
Hartville, OH 44632
216-877-3694

Hebron Community, Inc.
P.O. Box 11
Lawrenceville, VA 23868

Hope House Foundation
100 W. Plume St., Suite 224
Norfolk, VA 23510
757-625-6161

Horizons Specialized
Services, Inc.
405 Oak St.
Steamboat Springs, CO
80477-4867
303-879-4466

Kensington Community
Corporation for Individual
Dignity
5425 Oxford Ave.
Philadelphia, PA 19124
215-288-9797

Mountain Valley
Developmental Services
P.O. Box 338
Glenwood Springs, CO
81602
970-945-2306

Mt. Angel Training Center
and Residential Services
P.O. Box 78
Mt. Angel, OR 97362
503-845-9214

New Opportunities
1400 Seventh St.
Madison, IL 62060
618-876-3178

Nia Comprehensive Center
for Developmental
Disabilities
1808 S. State St.
Chicago, IL 60616
312-949-1808
800-NIA-1976

Opportunities for
Handicapped, Inc.
3340 Marysville Blvd.
Sacramento, CA 95838
916-925-3522

Orange County Association
for the Help of Retarded
Citizens
249 Broadway
Newburgh, NY 12550
914-561-0670

Outlook Nashville, Inc.
3004 Tuggle Ave.
Nashville, TN 37211
615-834-7570

Phoenix Services, Inc.
1 Cumberland St.
Lebanon, PA 17042
717-270-1222

Pleasant View Homes, Inc.
P.O. Box 426
Broadway, VA 22815
540-896-8255

Primrose Center
2733 S. Fern Creek Ave.
Orlando, FL 32806-5591
407-898-7201

Project Independence of
Queens
88-11 169th St., 2nd Fl.
Jamaica, NY 11432
718-657-1739

RocVale Children's Home
4450 N. Rockton Ave.
Rockford, IL 61103
815-654-3050

San Antonio State School
P.O. Box 14700
San Antonio, TX 78214-0700
210-532-0700

Society to Aid Retarded,
Inc. (S.T.A.R.)
P.O. Box 1075
Torrance, CA 90505

Southwest Human
Development
202 E. Earll Dr., Suite 140
Phoenix, AZ 85012
602-266-5976

St. Joseph Home, Inc.
1226 S. Sunbury Rd.
Westerville, OH 43081-9105

Swift County Developmental
Achievement Center
2135 Minnesota Ave., Bldg. 1
Benson, MN 56215
320-843-4201

DISABLED, PHYSICALLY

Access to Independence, Inc.,
1310 Mendota St.
Madison, WI 53714-1039

A+ Home Care, Inc.
8932 Old Cedar Ave. S.
Bloomington, MN 55425
800-603-7760

Creative Recreation in
Special Populations, Inc.
(CRISP)
P.O. Box 1086
Fort Collins, CO 80522
970-493-4454

Disabled American Veterans
P.O. Box 14301
Cincinnati, OH 45250-0301
606-441-7300

Dystonia Support System
P.O. Box 21367
Cleveland, OH 44121-0367
216-321-4137

Getabout
P.O. Box 224
New Canaan, CT 06840-0224
203-966-1881

Greener Globe
600 Treese Way
Roseville, CA 95678
916-774-6498

Independence Crossroads
8932 Old Cedar Ave. S.
Bloomington, MN 55425
612-854-8004

Michigan Wheelchair
Athletic Association
P.O. Box 1455
Troy, MI 48099
810-979-8253
michwaa@juno.com

Mower Council for the
Handicapped
111 N. Main St.
Austin, MN 55912-3404
507-433-9609

San Francisco Committee for
Aid of Russian Disabled
Veterans
651 11th Ave.
San Francisco, CA 94118-3612

Southwestern Independent
Living Center
843 N. Main St.
Jamestown, NY 14701
716-661-3010

Special People, Inc.
Human Resources
City Hall
1420 Miner St.
Des Plaines, IL 60016

United Amputee Services
P.O. Box 4277
Winter Park, FL 32793
407-678-2920
vprice@magicnet.net

DISABLED, PHYSICALLY/
DEVELOPMENTALLY

Alaska Services for Enabling
Technology
P.O. Box 6485
Sitka, AK 99835
907-747-7615

Be an Angel Fund
T.H. Rogers School
5840 San Felipe
Houston, TX 77057
713-917-3568

Carroll County Health and
Home Care Services
Carroll County Complex
Ossipee, NH 03864
800-499-4171

Comprehensive Advocacy,
Inc.
4477 Emerald, Suite B-100
Boise, ID 83706-2044
800-632-5125

Disability Rights Education
& Defense Fund (DREDF)
2212 Sixth St.
Berkeley, CA 94710
510-644-2555

Disabled Resource Services
424 Pine St., Suite 101
Fort Collins, CO 80524-2421
970-482-2700

Families Helping Families at
the Crossroads of Louisiana
P.O. Box 12964
Alexandria, LA 71315-2964
318-445-7900
800-259-7200

F.A.M.I.L.Y. One-on-One
Services
P.O. Box 92
W. Jordan, UT 84084
801-268-6929

Friends of the
Handicapped, Inc.
P.O. Box 29
Perkasie, PA 18944
215-257-8732

Heartland Opportunity
Center
Madera Center
323 N. E St.
Madera, CA 93638-3245
209-674-8828

Hodan Center, Inc.
941 W. Fountain St.
P.O. Box 212
Mineral Point, WI 53565
608-987-3336

Humboldt Community
Access and Resource Center
(HCAR)
P.O. Box 2010
Eureka, CA 95502

Indiana Rehabilitation
Association
P.O. Box 44174
Indianapolis, IN 46244-0174
317-264-1222

Lifegains, Inc.
1601 S. Sterling St.
P.O. Drawer 1569
Morganton, NC 28680-1569
704-255-8845

Maidstone Foundation, Inc.
1225 Broadway
New York, NY 10001
212-889-5760

Maine Independent Living
Services, Inc.
424 Western Ave.
Augusta, ME 04330-6014
800-499-5434

North Country Center for
Independence
159 Margaret St., Suite 202
Plattsburgh, NY 12901
518-563-9058
ncci@slic.com

Open Door, Inc.
1445 S.E. Crystal Lake Dr.
Corvallis, OR 97333
503-752-9724

Options Center for
Independent Living
61 Meadowview Center
Kankakee, IL 60901
815-936-0100

Ozarks Valley Community
Service, Inc. (OVCS)
135 S. Main
Ironton, MO 63650-0156
573-546-2418

POWERS Coalition
P.O. Box 618
Sterling, VA 20167

Project Independence of
Eastern Connecticut
401 W. Thames St.
Unit 1601
Norwich, CT 06360
203-886-0677

Rehabilitation Center
1439 Buffalo St.
Olean, NY 14760
716-372-8909

Resource Center for
Accessible Living, Inc.
602 Albany Ave.
Kingston, NY 12401
914-331-0541

Riverfront Foundation
944 Green Bay St.
La Crosse, WI 54601
608-784-9450

Rockingham Opportunities
342 Cherokee Camp Rd.
Reidsville, NC 27320
336-342-4761

Sheltered Workshop
P.O. Box 2002
Clarksburg, WV 26302-2002
304-623-3757

Society Assisted Living (SAL)
4283 Paradise Rd.
Seville, OH 44273
330-725-7041
330-336-2045

Southwest Center for
Independent Living
1856 E. Cinderella
Springfield, MO 65804
800-676-7245

Specialized Training for
Adult Rehabilitation
(START)
20 N. 13th St.
Murphysboro, IL 62966-0938
618-687-2378

Turn Community Services
P.O. Box 1287
Salt Lake City, UT 84110-1287
801-359-8876

Vocational Services, Inc.
(VSI)
115 Blue Jay Dr.
Liberty, MO 64068
816-781-6292

VOLAR Center for
Independent Living
8929 Viscount, Suite 101
El Paso, TX 79225
915-591-0800
Volar1@whc.net

Waukesha Training Center
300 S. Prairie
Waukesha, WI 53186
414-547-6821

Western Carolina Center
Foundation, Inc.
P.O. Box 646
Morganton, NC 28680-0646
704-433-2862

Windhorse Foundation
1614 Camp Springs Rd.
Reidsville, NC 27320
910-969-9590

Workshop/Northeast Career
Planning
339 Broadway
Menards, NY 12204
518-463-8051

ELDERLY

Aging & Disabled Services,
Inc.
811 S. Palmer Ave.
Box 142
Georgiana, AL 36033

Beth Haven
2500 Pleasant St.
Hannibal, MO 63401
573-221-6000

Carroll County Health and
Home Care Services
Carroll County Complex
Ossipee, NH 03864
800-499-4171

Creative Recreation in
Special Populations, Inc.
(CRISP)
P.O. Box 1086
Fort Collins, CO 80522
970-493-4454

DARTS
1645 Marthaler La.
W. St. Paul, MN 55118
612-455-1560

Getabout
P.O. Box 224
New Canaan, CT 06840-0224
203-966-1881

Prairie Mission Retirement
Village
242 Carroll St.
R.R. 1, Box 1Z
St. Paul, KS 66771
316-449-2400

Project Independence of
Eastern Connecticut
401 W. Thames St.
Unit 1601
Norwich, CT 06360
203-886-0677

Wesley Heights
580 Long Hill Ave.
Shelton, CT 06484
203-929-5396

EMOTIONAL,
BEHAVIORAL DISORDERS

AIM Center
1903 McCallie Ave.
Chattanooga, TN 37404
615-624-4800

Burke Foundation
20800 Farm Rd. 150 W.
Driftwood, TX 78619
512-858-4258

Crestwood Children's
Center
2075 Scottsville Rd.
Rochester, NY 14623-2098
716-436-4442

Federation of Families for
Children's Mental Health
1021 Prince St.
Alexandria, VA 22314-2971
703-864-7710
www.ffcmh.org

Lake Whatcom Center
3400 Agate Heights
Bellingham, WA 98226
360-676-6000

Parents and Children
Coping Together
308 W. Broad St.
Richmond, VA 23220-4219
804-225-0002
800-788-0097

Rimrock Foundation
1231 N. 29th St.
Billings, MT 59101
800-227-3953

Staten Island Mental Health
Society, Inc.
669 Castleton Ave.
Staten Island, NY 10301
718-442-2225

Timberlawn Psychiatric
Research Foundation, Inc.
P.O. Box 270789
Dallas, TX 75227-0789
214-388-0451

TRANSACT Health Systems
of Central Pennsylvania
90 Beaver Dr.
DuBois, PA 15801
814-371-0414

Youth Services for
Oklahoma County
201 N.E. 50th St.
Oklahoma City, OK 73105-1811
405-235-7537

HOME CARE/MEALS

Bronx Home Care Services,
Inc.
3956 Bronxwood Ave.
Bronx, NY 10466
718-231-6292

Mobile Meals, Inc.
368 S. Main St.
Akron, OH 44311-1014
330-376-7717
800-TLC-MEAL

KIDNEY

*American Kidney Fund
6110 Executive Blvd.
Suite 1010
Rockville, MD 20852
800-638-8299
www.arbon.com/kidney/home.htm

MISCELLANEOUS

American Fund for
Alternatives to Animal
Research
175 W. 12th St., Suite 16G
New York, NY 10011-8220
212-989-8073

American Leprosy Missions
1 ALM Way
Greenville, SC 29601
800-543-3135
www.leprosy.org

American Spinal Research
Foundation
900 E. Tasman Dr.
San Jose, CA 95134
408-944-6066

American Vitiligo Research
Foundation, Inc.
P.O. Box 7540
Clearwater, FL 33758
727-461-3899

Colostomy Society of New
York
G.P.O. Box 517
New York, NY 10016
212-221-1246

*Endometriosis Association
8585 N. 76th Place
Milwaukee, WI 53223
414-355-2200

Floating Hospital
Pier 11, East River at Wall St.
New York, NY 10005
212-514-7440

Greater Erie Eye and Organ
Bank, Inc.
5015 Richmond St.
Erie, PA 16509-1949
814-866-3545

MCS Referral and Resources
(Multiple Chemical
Sensitivity)
508 Westgate Rd.
Baltimore, MD 21229-2343
410-448-3319
donnaya@rtk.net

National Stuttering Project
5100 E. LaPalma Ave.
Suite 208
Anaheim Hills, CA 92807
714-693-7480
800-364-1677

Thyroid Society
7515 S. Main St., Suite 545
Houston, TX 77030
800-THYROID
www.the-thyroid-society.org

Transplantation Society of
Michigan
2203 Platt Rd.
Ann Arbor, MI 48104
800-247-7250

Vulvar Pain Foundation
P.O. Drawer 177
Graham, NC 27253
910-226-0704

PARALYSIS

Spinal Cord Injury Network
International
3911 Princeton Dr.
Santa Rosa, CA 95405
800-548-CORD
www.sonic.net/~spinal/
spinal@sonic.net

STROKE

Palm Springs Stroke Activity
Center
P.O. Box 355
Palm Springs, CA 92263-0355
619-323-7676
PsStrkCntr@aol.com

Stroke Survivors Support Group of Pueblo
710½ E. Mesa Ave.
Pueblo, CO 81006
719-583-8498

SUBSTANCE ABUSE

Center for Creative Alternatives
1700 Adams, Suite 201
Costa Mesa, CA 92626
714-437-9535

Family Service Association
31 W. Market St.
Wilkes-Barre, PA 18701-1304
717-823-5144

Friendly Hand Foundation
347 S. Normandie Ave.
Los Angeles, CA 90020
213-389-9964

Highland Waterford Center, Inc.
4501 Grange Hall Rd.
Holly, MI 48442
810-634-0140

Prevention of Alcohol Problems, Inc.
4616 Longfellow Ave. S.
Minneapolis, MN 55407
612-729-3047

Samaritan Recovery Community, Inc.
319 S. Fourth St.
Nashville, TN 37206
615-244-4802

TRAUMA/INJURY

Brain Injury Association of Florida, Inc.
201 E. Sample Rd.
Pompano Beach, FL 33064
954-786-2400

Trauma Foundation
San Francisco General Hospital
Bldg. 1, Rm. 1, 1001 Protrero
San Francisco, CA 94110
415-821-8209

VETERANS

American Veteran's Relief Fund, Inc.
5930E Royal La.
Dallas, TX 75230-3849
214-696-3784

Disabled American Veterans
P.O. Box 14301
Cincinnati, OH 45250-0301
606-441-7300

Help Hospitalized Veterans
2065 Kurtz St.
San Diego, CA 92110
619-291-5846

San Francisco Committee for Aid of Russian Disabled Veterans
651 11th Ave.
San Francisco, CA 94118-3612

COOKING WITH PETA

A new cookbook from the authors of The Compassionate Cook,

featuring cover art by vegetarian artist Peter Max.

If you thought being a vegetarian meant going hungry, then you obviously haven't seen the folks from PETA eat!

PETA staffers not only love animals, they also love food—and this new cookbook is filled with their favorite vegan (containing no animal products) dishes. Recipes range from animal-free variations on "Mom's" cooking—like Tasty "Toona" Salad, Beefless Stew, Tofu Not-a-Turkey, and Chewy Chocolate Chip Cookies—to exotic new delights, like Elegant Eggplant Crostini, Sherried Portobellos, Lucky Luau Kebabs, and Amazing Apple and Date Mousse.

In addition to more than 200 recipes, the book includes information on how and why to go veggie, plus tips on replacing eggs and dairy products in cooking, using "mock meats," and cooking healthful, vegan foods that kids will actually eat.

Order Your Copy Today!

Send $20.90, check or money order (postage included), to: PETA Merchandise, 501 Front St., Norfolk, VA 23510. For credit card orders, call 1-800-483-4366.

"AN EXCELLENT COLLECTION FOR PEOPLE WHO WANT TO DECREASE OR ELIMINATE ANIMAL PRODUCTS IN THEIR DIETS ..."
—Carol Cubberley, Library Journal

"DELICIOUS RECIPES ..."
—Aquarius

"IT'S EASY TO 'LIVE AND LET LIVE' AND THIS BOOK WILL SHOW YOU HOW."
—Ingrid Newkirk, President, People for the Ethical Treatment of Animals

"TRY OUT THE RECIPES IN THIS BOOK. HAVE FUN AS YOU EXPERIMENT WITH DELIGHTFUL NEW TASTES AND HEALTHFUL INGREDIENTS."
—Neal Barnard, President, Physicians Committee for Responsible Medicine

---

PeTA PEOPLE FOR THE ETHICAL TREATMENT OF ANIMALS
501 Front St., Norfolk, VA 23510 • 757-622-PETA • www.peta-online.org

HEALTH CHARITIES THAT TEST ON ANIMALS

What Types of Charities Are on the "Do Test" List?

Health charities that conduct or fund experiments on animals are included on the "do test" list. These organizations deal with human health issues ranging from lung cancer to drug addiction to blindness. While some do have relevant and effective projects that help improve lives, all of them drain money away from these projects and into cruel experiments on animals. They starve, cripple, burn, poison, and slice open animals to study human diseases and disabilities. Such experiments have no practical benefit to anyone. They are unnecessary, unreliable, and sometimes dangerously misleading. "Enormous variations exist among rats, rabbits, dogs, pigs, and human beings, and meaningful scientific conclusions cannot be drawn about one species by studying another," says Neal Barnard, M.D. "Non-animal methods provide a more accurate method of testing and can be interpreted more objectively."

What Can Be Done to Stop Charities From Experimenting on Animals?

Many charities know that we can improve treatments through modern, non-animal methods, and they fund only non-animal research, leading to real progress in the prevention and treatment of disease. The next time you receive a donation request from a health charity, ask if it funds animal tests. Let charities know that you only give to organizations that alleviate suffering, not contribute to it.

* * *

Please note that most colleges and universities have laboratories that conduct animal experiments for health and other purposes. If you would like to know whether a specific school has an animal laboratory, please contact PETA. For information on the experiments being conducted and to voice your opinion, please contact the school.

* * *

The following health charities and service organizations DO conduct or fund animal experiments. They may deal with several issues, including nonhealth-related issues, but they are listed according to their primary health focus. Listed in parentheses are affiliated organizations that may or may not fund animal experiments. For more information on the programs and activities of an organization, please contact the organization or PETA.

112

AIDS/HIV

**American Foundation for
AIDS Research (AMFAR),**
733 Third Ave., 12th Fl.
New York, NY 10017
800-39-AMFAR

Pediatric AIDS Foundation
1311 Colorado Ave.
Santa Monica, CA 90404
310-395-9051

ALZHEIMER'S DISEASE

Alzheimer's Association
919 N. Michigan Ave.
Suite 1000
Chicago, IL 60611-1676
312-335-8700

**Alzheimer's Disease
Research**
15825 Shady Grove Rd.
Suite 140
Rockville, MD 20850
800-437-AHAF

ARTHRITIS

Arthritis Foundation
1330 W. Peachtree St.
Atlanta, GA 30309
404-872-7100

BIRTH DEFECTS

**March of Dimes Birth
Defects Foundation**
1275 Mamaroneck Ave.
White Plains, NY 10605
914-997-4504

**Muscular Dystrophy
Association**
3300 E. Sunrise Dr.
Tucson, AZ 85718-3208
800-572-1717

**Shriners Hospitals for
Crippled Children**
International Shrine
Headquarters
2900 Rocky Point Dr.
Tampa, FL 33607
813-281-0300

United Cerebral Palsy
1660 L St. N.W., Suite 700
Washington, DC 20036
202-776-0406

BLIND, VISUALLY
IMPAIRED

**Foundation Fighting
Blindness**
Executive Plaza One
11350 McCormick Rd.
Suite 800
Hunt Valley, MD 21031-1014
410-785-1414

**Massachusetts Lions Eye
Research Fund (Lions Club
International Foundation)**
118 Allen St.
Hampden, MA 01036
413-566-3756

**Research to Prevent
Blindness**
645 Madison Ave., 21st Fl.
New York, NY 10022-1010
800-621-0026

BLOOD

American Red Cross
430 17th St. N.W.
Washington, DC 20006
202-737-8300

**Leukemia Society of
America**
600 Third Ave.
New York, NY 10016
212-573-8484

**National Hemophilia
Foundation**
110 Greene St.
Suite 303
New York, NY 10012
212-219-8180

BURNS

Shriners Burn Institute
International Shrine
Headquarters
2900 Rocky Point Dr.
Tampa, FL 33607
813-281-0300

CANCER

American Cancer Society
1599 Clifton Rd. N.E.
Atlanta, GA 30329
404-320-3333

**American Institute for
Cancer Research**
1759 R St. N.W.
Washington, DC 20009
202-328-7744

**Cancer Research
Foundation of America**
200 Daingerfield Rd.
Suite 200
Alexandria, VA 22314
703-836-4412

City of Hope
208 W. Eighth St.
Los Angeles, CA 90014
213-626-4611

**Leukemia Society of
America**
600 Third Ave.
New York, NY 10016
212-573-8484

**Memorial Sloan-Kettering
Cancer Center**
1275 York Ave.
New York, NY 10021
212-639-2000

**National Foundation for
Cancer Research**
7315 Wisconsin Ave.
Suite 500W
Bethesda, MD 20814
800-321-2873

Nina Hyde Center for Breast
Cancer Research
Lombardi Cancer Research
Center
3800 Reservoir Rd. N.W.
Washington, DC 20007
202-687-4597

St. Jude Children's Research
Hospital
501 St. Jude Place
Memphis, TN 38105
901-522-9733

Susan G. Komen Breast
Cancer Foundation
5005 LBJ Freeway, Suite 370
Dallas, TX 75244
972-855-1600
800-462-9273

CHILDREN

Boys Town National
Research Hospital
555 N. 30th St.
Omaha, NE 68131
402-498-6511

Juvenile Diabetes
Foundation International
120 Wall St.
New York, NY 10005-4001
800-JDF-CURE
www.jdfcure.com

Pediatric AIDS Foundation
1311 Colorado Ave.
Santa Monica, CA 90404
310-395-9051

Shriners Hospitals for
Crippled Children
International Shrine
Headquarters
2900 Rocky Point Dr.
Tampa, FL 33607
813-281-0300

Society for Pediatric
Pathology
6278 Old McLean Village Dr.
McLean, VA 22101
703-556-9222

St. Jude Children's Research
Hospital
501 St. Jude Place
Memphis, TN 38105
901-522-9733

Sudden Infant Death
Syndrome Alliance
1314 Bedford Ave.
Suite 210
Baltimore, MD 21208
800-221-SIDS

DEAF/HEARING-IMPAIRED

Boys Town National
Research Hospital
555 N. 30th St.
Omaha, NE 68131
402-498-6511

DIABETES

American Diabetes
Association
1660 Duke St.
Alexandria, VA 22314
703-549-1500

Joslin Diabetes Center
One Joslin Place
Boston, MA 02215
617-732-2400

Juvenile Diabetes
Foundation International
120 Wall St.
New York, NY 10005-4001
800-JDF-CURE
www.jdfcure.com

ELDERLY

American Federation for
Aging Research
1414 Ave. of the Americas
18th Fl.
New York, NY 10019
212-752-2327

EMOTIONAL/BEHAVIORAL
DISORDERS

National Alliance for
Research of Schizophrenia
and Depression
60 Cutter Mill Rd.
Suite 200
Great Neck, NY 11021
516-829-0091

National Alliance for the
Mentally Ill
200 N. Glebe Rd.
Suite 1015
Arlington, VA 22203-3754
703-524-7600

EPILEPSY

Epilepsy Foundation of
America
4351 Garden City Dr.
Suite 500
Landover, MD 20785
301-459-3700

HEART

American Heart Association
7272 Greenville Ave.
Dallas, TX 75231-4596
214-373-6300

Coronary Heart Disease
Research
15825 Shady Grove Rd.
Suite 140
Rockville, MD 20850
800-437-AHAF

KIDNEY

National Kidney Foundation
30 E. 33rd St.
New York, NY 10016
212-889-2210

LUNG

American Lung Association
1740 Broadway
New York, NY 10019
212-315-8700

MISCELLANEOUS

Amyotrophic Lateral Sclerosis Association
21021 Ventura Blvd.
Suite 321
Woodland Hills, CA 91364
818-340-7500

Crohn's & Colitis Foundation of America
386 Park Ave. S.
New York, NY 10016-8804
800-932-8804
www.ccfa.org

Cystic Fibrosis Foundation
6931 Arlington Rd.
Bethesda, MD 20814
800-FIGHT-CF

Families of Spinal Muscular Atrophy
P.O. Box 196
Libertyville, IL 60048-0196
800-886-1762
www.fsma.org
sma@interaccess.com

Huntington's Disease Society of America
744 Dulaney Valley Rd.
Suite 17
Towson, MD 21204
410-823-8766

International Foundation for Gastrointestinal Disorders
P.O. Box 17864
Milwaukee, WI 53217
414-964-1799

National Headache Foundation
428 W. St. James Place, 2nd Fl.
Chicago, IL 60614-2750
800-843-2256

National Multiple Sclerosis Society
733 Third Ave., 6th Fl.
New York, NY 10017-3288
212-986-3240

National Psoriasis Foundation
6600 S.W. 92nd Ave.
Suite 300
Portland, OR 97223-7195
503-244-7404

National Vitiligo Foundation
P.O. Box 6337
Tyler, TX 75711

Tourette Syndrome Association
42-40 Bell Blvd.
Bayside, NY 11361-2820
800-237-0717
tourette@ix.netcom.com

PARALYSIS

American Paralysis Foundation
500 Morris Ave.
Springfield, NJ 07081
201-379-2690

Eastern Paralyzed Veterans Association
7 Mill Brook Rd.
Wilton, NH 03086
603-654-5511

Miami Project to Cure Paralysis
P.O. Box 016960, R-48
Miami, FL 33101
305-243-6001

Paralyzed Veterans of America
801 18th St. N.W.
Washington, DC 20006-3715
202-872-1300

PARKINSON'S DISEASE

American Parkinson Disease Association
1250 Hylan Blvd.
Staten Island, NY 10305
800-223-2732

National Parkinson Foundation
1501 N.W. Ninth Ave.
Miami, FL 33136
800-327-4545

Parkinson's Disease Foundation
710 W. 168th St.
New York, NY 10032-9982
212-923-4700

United Parkinson Foundation
833 W. Washington Blvd.
Chicago, IL 60607
312-733-1893

STROKE

National Stroke Association
96 Inverness Dr. E., Suite I
Englewood, CO 80112-5112
800-STROKES

VETERANS

Eastern Paralyzed Veterans Association
7 Mill Brook Rd.
Wilton, NH 03086
603-654-5511

Paralyzed Veterans of America
801 18th St. N.W.
Washington, DC 20006-3715
202-872-1300

DON'T JUST PAY THEM... *Enlighten them*

PETA Check Series & Matching Address Labels

Hemp Checkbook Cover w/*light blue* embroidered PETA logo

PETA "Respect Your Fellow Earthlings" Checks, Address Labels and Checkbook Cover *by Berke Breathed*

ALL ITEMS in FULL COLOR!

········· ORDER FORM ·········

IMPORTANT! Include the following with this form:

❏ Re-order form from present checks OR voided check.
   Include **starting number #**_____ and any changes.
❏ Deposit ticket from the same account.
❏ Payment choice:
   ❏ Automatically debit my checking account
   ❏ Check made payable to **Message!Products™**
   ❏ Charge to: ❏ Visa®   ❏ MasterCard®
                 ❏ American Express® ❏ Discover®

Account Number_____ Exp. Date ___/___

Signature_____

❏ Three lines of address personalization for address labels, if applicable:

_____
_____
_____

❏ Daytime Phone Number (____) _____

CONFIDENTIAL! In case of questions about your order only.

Check Price .... $_____	

PETA Series
❏ 200 Singles $15.95 (PSSS) ❏ 150 Duplicates $17.95 (PSDS)

Respect Your Fellow Earthlings Checks
❏ 200 Singles $13.95 (BBSS) ❏ 150 Duplicates $14.95 (BBDS)

240 Labels – Price .... $_____
❏ PETA Series Labels $12.95 ❏ "Respect..." Labels $9.95

Checkbook Cover Price .... $_____
❏ Embroidered Hemp Cover $14.95 ❏ "Respect..." Cover $11.95

MN residents only add 6.5% tax .... $_____

Shipping & Handling .... $_____
❏ $1.95 per item or ❏ *First Class* $3.95 per item

TOTAL. .... $_____

XF

**PETA'S
2000
Shopping
Guide for
Caring
Consumers**
Redeemable
through
company only.

**PETA'S
2000
Shopping
Guide for
Caring
Consumers**
Redeemable
through
company only.

**PETA'S
2000
Shopping
Guide for
Caring
Consumers**
Redeemable
through
company only.

**PETA'S
2000
Shopping
Guide for
Caring
Consumers**
Redeemable
through
company only.

**PETA'S
2000
Shopping
Guide for
Caring
Consumers**
Redeemable
through
company only.

**PETA'S
2000
Shopping
Guide for
Caring
Consumers**
Redeemable
through
company only.

**PETA'S
2000
Shopping
Guide for
Caring
Consumers**
Redeemable
through
company only.

**PETA'S
2000
Shopping
Guide for
Caring
Consumers**
Redeemable
through
company only.

PETA'S 2000 Shopping Guide for Caring Consumers
Redeemable through company only.

PETA'S 2000 Shopping Guide for Caring Consumers
Redeemable through company only.

PETA'S 2000 Shopping Guide for Caring Consumers
Redeemable through company only.

PETA'S 2000 Shopping Guide for Caring Consumers
Redeemable through company only.

PETA'S 2000 Shopping Guide for Caring Consumers
Redeemable through company only.

PETA'S 2000 Shopping Guide for Caring Consumers
Redeemable through company only.

PETA'S 2000 Shopping Guide for Caring Consumers
Redeemable through company only.

PETA'S 2000 Shopping Guide for Caring Consumers
Redeemable through company only.

**PETA'S
2000
Shopping
Guide for
Caring
Consumers**
Redeemable
through
company only.

**PETA'S
2000
Shopping
Guide for
Caring
Consumers**
Redeemable
through
company only.

**PETA'S
2000
Shopping
Guide for
Caring
Consumers**
Redeemable
through
company only.

**PETA'S
2000
Shopping
Guide for
Caring
Consumers**
Redeemable
through
company only.

**PETA'S
2000
Shopping
Guide for
Caring
Consumers**
Redeemable
through
company only.

**PETA'S
2000
Shopping
Guide for
Caring
Consumers**
Redeemable
through
company only.

**PETA'S
2000
Shopping
Guide for
Caring
Consumers**
Redeemable
through
company only.

**PETA'S
2000
Shopping
Guide for
Caring
Consumers**
Redeemable
through
company only.

PETA'S 2000 Shopping Guide for Caring Consumers
Redeemable through company only.

PETA'S 2000 Shopping Guide for Caring Consumers
Redeemable through company only.

PETA'S 2000 Shopping Guide for Caring Consumers
Redeemable through company only.

PETA'S 2000 Shopping Guide for Caring Consumers
Redeemable through company only.

PETA'S 2000 Shopping Guide for Caring Consumers
Redeemable through company only.

PROJECT

PETA'S 2000 Shopping Guide for Caring Consumers
Redeemable through company only.

PROJECT

PETA'S 2000 Shopping Guide for Caring Consumers
Redeemable through company only.

PETA'S 2000 Shopping Guide for Caring Consumers
Redeemable through company only.

PROJECT

**PETA'S
2000
Shopping
Guide for
Caring
Consumers**
Redeemable
through
company only.

PROJECT

**PETA'S
2000
Shopping
Guide for
Caring
Consumers**
Redeemable
through
company only.

PROJECT

**PETA'S
2000
Shopping
Guide for
Caring
Consumers**
Redeemable
through
company only.

PROJECT

**PETA'S
2000
Shopping
Guide for
Caring
Consumers**
Redeemable
through
company only.

What Is PETA?

People for the Ethical Treatment of Animals (PETA) is an international nonprofit organization dedicated to exposing and eliminating all animal abuse. PETA uses public education, litigation, research and investigations, media campaigns, and involvement at the grassroots level to accomplish this goal.

With the help of our dedicated members, PETA persuades major corporations to stop testing products on animals; advocates alternatives to eating animals by promoting a vegetarian diet; and has forced the closure of federally funded animal research facilities because of animal abuses.

To help stop the exploitation and abuse of animals, become a PETA member today.

MEMBERSHIP & DONATION FORM

Enclosed is my contribution to go toward your vital work in behalf of all animals.

☐ $16 ☐ $25 ☐ $50 ☐ $100 ☐ Other $ _____

(Annual membership is $16.00. Members recieve PETA's *Guide to Compassionate Living* and a subscription to PETA's quarterly newsletter.)

☐ I'm already a PETA member. This is an extra donation.

Name _____

Address _____

City _____ State _____ Zip _____

Complete this form and send with your check to:

PETA 501 Front St., Norfolk, VA 23510

Thank you from all of us at PETA.

Ask your store to carry these books:

Vegan Vittles
A collection of recipies inspired by the critters of Farm Sanctuary. Includes photos and biographies of resident animals.

$11.95

Meatless Burgers
Juicy, chewy, mouth-watering burgers of beans, grains and vegetables.

$9.95

Delicious Food for a Healthy Heart
Over 120 Cholesterol-Free, Low-Fat, Quick & Easy Recipes.

$12.95

Becoming Vegetarian
Three vegetarian dieticians present the latest nutritional information for optimal health and kindness.

$15.95

Warming Up to Living Foods
Zesty, creative, nutritious dishes made from raw and living foods.

$15.95

Peaceful Palate
Quality vegan fare for the novice or veteran cook.

$15.00

or you may order directly from:

The Book Publishing Company
P.O. Box 99
Summertown, TN 38483

Or call: 1-800-695-2241
Please add $2.50 per book for shipping.